Those Who Can't

A Danger to Themselves and Others

by Patrick Nichols

Cover photo by Dr. Claire Prouve
Cover and interior design by Vinnie Corbo

Published by Volossal Publishing
www.volossal.com

Copyright © 2022
ISBN 979-8-9850796-3-0

This book may not be reproduced or resold in whole or in part through print, electronic or any other medium. All rights reserved.

Table of Contents

Introduction - LOST	7
Chapter One - Death on the Job	11
Chapter Two - Learning the Ropes	17
Chapter Three - The Check is in the Mail	33
Chapter Four - Reputation vs. Experience	47
Chapter Five - You Can't Teach	65
Chapter Six - The Parallax View	83
Chapter Seven - Peter Has No Principles	97
Chapter Eight - Losing Everything	107
Chapter Nine - Teaching Wasn't Always This Way	119
Chapter Ten - Second Chances	139
Chapter Eleven - Measure This	153
Chapter Twelve - Investigations	175
Chapter Thirteen - Personal Demons	179
Chapter Fourteen - To Be or Not to Be	193
Chapter Fifteen - Endings	209
About The Author	213

For Yudelfi

LOST

It's easy to fall back on the years of humiliating beatings on the brick steps of my childhood home, when my mother set my father on me with a belt, and he stripped me naked, whipping me down the stairs, one at a time, as the reason why I became the man that I did. That ended when I was eight years old. Why did I continue to struggle my entire life?

As a child, I tested gifted. I dreamt of becoming an astronaut. Instead, I spent a lifetime hiding in dark places, working jobs no one wanted; I stood on the fringes of relationships because I had learned that intimacy at close quarters always resulted in abhorrent behavior on my part.

Even when I put down the drink, the drugs, I still behaved monstrously. Perhaps more so. Therapy, medication and everything else a person could immerse oneself in didn't relieve the anguish and the consequent unpredictable and disproportionately reactive behavior. Inevitably, I would reach back for the solutions which sort of worked, at least for a while -- despite how many years of "sobriety", of working a program, of therapy, I had had under my belt: I got drunk. And high. And a whole lot of other things. For as long and deeply as I could.

Most of my adult life, I worked with troubled teenagers as a NYC public high school teacher. Yet, I was a danger to myself and others and I knew it. Why couldn't I find the help that I needed with my education, intelligence, and all the resources at my disposal? I certainly tried often enough. Once I had the Director of Psychiatry at a major NY hospital where I had been seeking help for the better part of a year tell me that I'd run out of insurance "long before we ever figured out what was wrong with you." And why had so many others whose paths I'd crossed fatally self-destructed, sometimes before my eyes, when I had not?

I often felt helpless, as if an overwhelmingly but unfathomable outside force worked against me. The early childhood violence and my judgments against myself for having been the receptacle of these kinds of brutality formed the lens through which I experienced reality: I had learned to create the experience of the world from which I now recoiled. How had I become the author of this life? It seemed incomprehensible.

~

We are raised to "fit into" a society that will no longer exist by the time we become adults. Before we fully mature, we have woven into us a nearly undetectable emotional and psychological fabric, an overlay if you will, which frames almost all that we see and experience, and this interactive membrane amplifies the powerful forces, which drive us blindly, sometimes ruthlessly and unforgivingly. It's not what's happening that's the problem; it's the stories we are unwittingly telling ourselves about what's happening: it's the waking up of the unresolved emotional states hidden deep within us and the interplay between what our body is experiencing and how these narratives amplify our distress, which convincingly create the reality we often desperately struggle against. These "stories" we tell ourselves are the children of our emotional landscape, educated into us by our family, culture, religion, political ideology, schools, friends, and community. They are born of our undigested emotion, of our ungrieved losses, of our unhealed wounds.

~

If we don't elevate our understanding of what it means to be a human being, compassionately changing how we treat ourselves and each other, we condemn each successive generation to create monsters of their own out of a deep sense of being profoundly unfulfilled.

Education might better be reimagined as the nurturing and empowering of individuals from the time they are their most vulnerable until an age when they can bring forth a world that perhaps only the most inspired amongst us can imagine. If this is too much to reach for, then if only our education could sensitize us to this one simply truth, it might just be enough: When we hurt one of us, we hurt all of us. There is no "them." There is only "us." We are both the unarmed teen who's been mistakenly gunned down and the hand pulling the trigger; we are both the homeless man begging for an ounce of humanity and the passerby who cringes at his existence.

What's laid down on these pages is my story. Perhaps time and vulnerability have forever colored these experiences. Maybe I've even confused strong personal feelings about events for the events themselves. Irrespective of these realities and the many truths I may never know, this *is* my story, and I'm sticking to it.

- JP

Chapter One

Death on the Job

J*ust married, beginning a career as a teacher with no classroom training, already drinking heavily on Friday nights with bouts of cocaine use, I struggle to come out of weekends able to show up for a job, for school, for anything. I fight to get this job I believe no one wants, yet something about me warns others not to hire me. I am, at the time, already an honorably discharged veteran, a former police officer in the Air Force, where I fought and rejected authority until I nearly self destructed. And while my drinking hadn't taken off in the service, the emotional groundwork that would fuel my self destructive bouts had clearly risen to the surface.*

I am hired, but only after an officer from the then Board of Education threatens my future administrator. "You don't want this man, I'll find someone else who does. Now make up your mind." I believe this officer saw something in me the others didn't. He is black and I am white, but he recognizes there is something different about me beyond the clear sense that I am troubled. The administrator who doesn't want me is white. I am not his kind of white.

I am reminded of how I attempted to open up my own bank account in the early 1990's and being endlessly questioned. I had been a teacher for five years at this point and my wife and I were struggling.

I wanted to separate our finances as the only credit card I owned was through her.

It is summer and I enter the bank in the middle of the morning. The bank officer won't open the account for me, won't touch the thousands of dollars I placed on her desk, money which I've withdrawn from another bank where my account is linked to my wife's, won't accept my driver's license as ID. She keeps circling around something I don't understand, refusing me. A supervisor, a person of color, comes over and asks her, this white woman, what seems to be the problem, and she recoils as if I'm dirt, trying to explain to her supervisor without coming right out and saying why that they can't open an account for me. Her supervisor asks the one question the white woman never asked, "Do you have a job?"

I answer, "Yes. I'm a teacher."

"So you work for the Board of Education."

"Yes."

"For how long?"

"For five years."

The supervisor looks at the white woman as if she has somehow been inhumane. When the supervisor leaves, the white woman says to me, "Why didn't you tell me you have a job?" She is relieved now but still calming herself.

I answer, "Because you never asked."

No one bothers to ask. They look at me and they know. I'm not like them. I later recognize she believed I was a drug dealer.

With this job, this unrelenting and brutal responsibility to show up daily, to work attempting to educate incarcerated adolescents who seem no different than I have been, I am frightened more than ever.. My mind tells me this will become my career, my means of supporting the family I don't yet have. Each week gets more difficult. I miss days because I am hung over. I return shaken, but I continue.

I look into faces that could have been "my boys", could have been anyone I had grown up with. They are hopeless. I run into others from my neighborhood who know me -- only they are now locked up. I do not understand why I did not end up here. I fear one day I will.

~

The end of Christmas break during my third year of teaching returned us to a tragedy. One of my students had been killed. He had been the third student to die in three years. This would become the pattern for the first 15 years: I was to lose at least one student each year I taught. After that, the losses came in clusters. At the end of 27 years, the number would be considerable. Most often, these young men and women were murdered: shot or stabbed to death on a train, the streets, by rival gang members, by other teens trying to rob them or accidentally by a police officer.

Once, when I taught on Rikers Island, a student of mine had actually been killed inside the prison. It had been my second year of teaching, and I had lost only one other student at that point – a young man named Herbert who, shortly after his release from jail, had been stabbed to death in a moving subway car.

The disputes were always the same: someone had disrespected someone else; perhaps one kid wanted the other's coat or sneakers. The reason never mattered – maybe it even seemed completely senseless to you -- but for these young men and women, reputation and respect were often life and death issues. That's all you really needed to understand.

Kahlil, the second student whom I was to lose, had been scheduled for release on the day of his death, but what he didn't know was that the Department of Corrections had planned what they called a "turn-around." A Corrections Officer (CO) led Kahlil past the eight locked doors of the prison to the final door, which opened onto the street. Kahlil waited with the escorting CO in front of each door until it was opened and then locked behind him, as it was a rule in prison that two successive doors could not be opened at the same time.

You endured this grueling process each time you entered or left the facility. The most insidious section of your journey consisted of attempting to pass through a set of sliding doors that led along the perimeter of a glass encased control booth just up the stairs from the street.

Passage through the two doors worked like this: you'd wait patiently for a CO in this control hub to notice you. Hopefully, he would then press a button that caused the first door to slide open. At this point, you would enter the slim corridor that led along the glass enclosed control center. Once you entered this corridor, the first door closed behind you, leaving you locked in. Only then could the second door at the far end of this narrow passageway be opened, allowing you entrance into the main facility. Regularly, people working in this control hub mysteriously forgot about you after closing the first door, leaving you trapped between the two locked doors.

On the outside of the glass that looked into this hub, which contained upwards of eight working individuals, was a sign boldly declaring, "**DO NOT KNOCK ON GLASS.**" Of course, if you were a CO, this rule didn't apply. As a teacher, you simply waited. If you exhibited impatience, you were completely ignored, sometimes for upwards of five minutes at a time. If you knocked on the glass, you were either further ignored or violently chastised, as if you were an idiot.

"Can't you FUCKING read?" And then you would be ignored some more.

When Kahlil was released through the second sliding door and had a view of the final door at the bottom of the stairs, he could see the two detectives waiting there for him. Of course, the CO escorted him down to the front door of the facility before releasing him into the custody of the two detectives who then "turned him around" and brought him back through the eight locked doors where he was charged with a new crime and re-introduced into the population. This little trick, a rare collaboration between two city organizations, allowed Law Enforcement to pressure an offender with the hopes of getting him to spill everything he knew on some other unsolved crime the police believed the youth might be connected to.

Kahlil, only 14 and very attached to his grandmother, found himself desperate to call home and let her know what had happened, both so that she shouldn't worry and in the hopes that she might somehow save him from this nightmare. In his frenzy, his heart now pumping wildly, he cut the phone line. In jail, there are a number of things that you never do: jumping the phone line is on the top of that list. The youth who Kahlil had crossed was not unsympathetic to Kahlil's plight, but he had to do something so as not to lose respect. Instead of punching Kahlil in the face, and leaving him marked, cut or bruised, the youth found compassion and directed a shot at the Kahlil's chest. No one knew that Kahlil had a heart murmur. In his excited and desperate state, the blow, not particularly hard, killed him.

That was a good day for the Department of Corrections: one dead and another, who had been scheduled for release in just four months, would end up serving extensive time for murder.

When we returned from Christmas break where I now taught in Bushwick, Brooklyn, it didn't take an hour for the entire school to know that Richard had shot himself in the head on Christmas morning. His best friend, who had witnessed the event, was also in my class, so I got to read about it in his journal. The story went like this:

Rich had been thrown out of his house. It wasn't the first time. His parents felt he was a bad influence on his younger brother. He loved that kid, but they saw it some other way. They didn't like the way he was living. So Rich spent the better part of Christmas Eve out on the street drinking "forties" (40 ounce Budweisers) and smoking "blunts" (marijuana). I joined him some time in the afternoon. He was already pretty wasted. He began playing around with a handgun, removing all the bullets and then pretending to play Russian Roulette. He'd spin the chambers and then place the gun to his head, pull the trigger and pretend to shoot himself.

I said, "Yo, Rich. Stop messing around."

He just kept loading and unloading the gun. At the end, he left a single bullet in one of the chambers.

We spoke about how hurt he felt being separated from his younger brother, especially on Christmas. When evening came, we was both pretty drunk. And when midnight rolled around, I didn't want to leave him alone, 'cause he didn't look right. So we kept drinking together.

Around two in the morning, he pulled out the revolver again. "You want to see something?" he said, spun the chamber and then put the pistol to his head, pulling the trigger. I didn't even have a chance to say anything to him. Whether he forgot about the single bullet or not, I couldn't say, but the gun went off. It seemed for a moment as if Rich was surprised. He struggled to say something, leaned against the wall of that hallway, before sliding down and dying.

When I pressed Johnny on it, he told me that he believed that Richard had simply forgotten that there was one bullet left in the gun.

That was the third student of mine to die, but I still didn't know it was to become a pattern, which would continue uninterrupted for the next 12 years.

Each time a student died, we felt it both as a school and individuals. Eventually, the collective weight of each of their deaths, the funerals, the bereaved families, the other grieving students -- all began to consume some part of me until I felt that teaching, perhaps, was too great a drain on the human spirit.

In year 10 of my teaching stint, a single death once set our entire school, which was located in Greenwich Village, into grieving. The boy had been shot down in the street for his sneakers. Many of us attended the funeral. A lot of silence that day. One of the results was the boy's mother set up a scholarship fund in memory of her son. Each year, she'd return during the June graduation and hand out a check to some lucky student. She'd give a short speech. All I saw was this poor woman who had outlived one of her children, forever lost in a spiral of grief, trying to regain her balance after this most unnatural act had crushed her. My colleagues and I spoke about how it remained painful to see her as her presence somehow awakened in us the tragedy of that loss, perhaps because it still lived within her. Her speeches got shorter and shorter. One year she simply never returned.

I thought about Richard that day as I walked home from the other student's funeral, taking the Brooklyn Bridge to clear my head. I remembered seeing Richard in the hallway after we'd asked him in the middle of some improvisations to go out and pretend to be an awkward nerd who was trying to solicit the autograph of a young woman who sat outside of the guidance office with her entourage. My student actors believed the girl to be Spinderella, a female hip hop artist, who needed a few credits to complete her high school diploma. It was the only time I'd ever seen Richard not convincingly perform a role I'd assigned him. Inside the room, he'd do it perfectly, looking like a contemporary Jerry Lewis, physical comedy and all, causing all of us to laugh so hard we could hardly breathe, but he could not pull it off in front of the girl. Instead, after an awkward silence, he just shook her hand.

When I asked him about it, he simply said, "She's somebody. I'm not going to make an ass out of myself in front of her."

Respect. We all want it. We all want to be seen, heard, and acknowledged. In Richard's mind, his family wanted to erase him, so that Christmas morning he did the job for them.

Chapter Two

Learning the Ropes

I *felt ashamed of myself -- not because of some one thing that I had done; rather, this feeling lived inside me, lying quietly beneath the surface, softly resonating in waves of self-loathing; other times, it became a bitter and endless voice crying out my personal truth, "YOU'RE A FUCKING LOSER!" These were the exact words that I sometimes heard screaming in my own head. Shame spoke to me as an intimate who knew me better than I could ever know myself. Unshakeable in me was the belief that it was only a matter of time before I would be exposed and humiliated, helpless to defend myself and my life, that my actual existence, my continued membership in the human race, would be lain me at the feet of the merciless. In the end, I would be discarded.*

~

The room moves as one, teenagers in monochromatic uniforms rising and opening up into a circle around one tall, slender young man and myself. He smiles nervously, drawing his arms apart in wide arcing motions as he wails comically in the badly dubbed intonations of a kung-fu movie action star.

"You killed my master." He says, his lips moving out of sync with his words. He is convincingly hilarious. The room, now a single entity, waits.

I am a teacher on Rikers Island, a prison for incarcerated adolescents in NYC, and my students, who are almost always completely out of control as it is my first year teaching, have just discovered that no so long ago I'd studied martial arts. One of them has chosen to confront me.

I study the boy in front of me and then put my hands down. I have no student-teaching experience; no one has ever taught me anything about how to teach: this is the first classroom I've ever stepped into where I wasn't a student. Yet I somehow know in this moment if I am to become their teacher, I will have to rely on something that even I have never believed in before: my authority as their teacher.

"Sit down," I hear my voice say. It is not a voice I know.

The young man continues, even more exaggerated than before in both tone and motion. I stand firm. He lurches forward, but I fight my hands as they begin to rise.

"I said, 'Sit down.'" This new voice is steady. He pauses to study me. The room holds its breath. A Correction Officer enters, but I wave him off. "Everything's fine in here. Just doing a little demonstration."

"Okay," he says, "but try quieting it down a bit."

The boy disarmed more by the moment than by me, slowly backs away, looks for a chair and then sits. The room disintegrates into individuals who find seats, and within moments the classroom is reassembled. I begin to teach, and for the first time in five months, I have full command of a room.

It is better than my first day of teaching on Rikers when my entire class consisted of two students: one with his head down on the desk and the other with his arms folded across his chest, his legs up on the table in front of him and his eyes locked tight.

Moments before, I had stood in the middle of a classroom filled with teachers and inmates, two correctional officers, the principal and her minions. Back then, principals had minions. My colleagues, much more seasoned than I, had quickly surveyed the situation and sought out the most promising individuals -- pockets of adolescent inmates who up until a moment ago never imagined they'd be in school while in prison. I watched in awe as they proceeded to teach. Many of their students were responding.

I still hadn't said a word to my two prospects. They were the leftovers. I had moved too slowly and found myself with the hard cases no one else had wanted or cared to approach. Although I didn't know it then, this would be my lot in teaching: My best work would be with the hard cases.

I felt embarrassed attempting to breach the silence with other people watching. What do you say to people who don't want you to speak to them? Days before, two teachers had quit although we hadn't yet met a single student. Just the Correction Officers' briefing combined with all the locked doors had been enough to scare them away -- that and being left alone in a corridor alongside a group of what appeared to be unsupervised adult inmates, a technique used to purposefully frighten us. The Department of Corrections simply didn't want us there. We were a threat to security, and they were right, only we were too naive and idealistic to grasp this simple reality.

I still hadn't spoken. The two teenagers sat still but tense with visibly tightened muscles, and I feared that anything I said might set them off, but the principal, who was hovering around the room surrounded by her entourage, had just set her sights on me.

I began speaking, at first really to no one in particular. Eventually, my rhetoric picked up rhythm and speed. Finally, one of them spoke.

"I wasn't going to school when I was in NY."

"Where are we now?" I asked.

"We's in jail, you idiot."

Teaching would be like that. I'd often be taught by my students. Despite the fact that territorially this institution existed within the geographic borders of New York City, jail was jail and it really wasn't anywhere. It was just jail.

Over the next two years, I'd learn how true this was. Jail existed in its own world with its own rules, and you couldn't survive on the inside being the person you had been on the outside. You had to become somebody else. And you could never tell the truth about anything, especially about yourself.

Near the end of my third year of teaching, I found myself wandering down a corridor of a building that I still didn't know when

Those Who Can't

I heard voices. No students clamored through the halls that day, so this lone venue just outside an empty lunchroom seemed unrecognizable. We had finished administering the last of the state exams only a day before, so now the teachers who weren't marking had cornered themselves in their rooms or vanished through side exits only to reappear miraculously just before sign out.

The voices grew louder and more passionate. I almost recognized one of them. "These idiots!" one roared. "How many times did I tell them how to do this and still they manage to fuck it up! This is 3rd grade math. Am I right? Why, this child must be retarded. That's it, I'm teaching the retarded!"

Laughter. "I know. I know. Jacquan is retarded." More laughter.

"This is going to take all day. I don't understand these kids. Didn't they learn anything?"

I peered through the window of the lunchroom door. Two of my colleagues were busy erasing answers for the recently administered state math exam.

"Here. Check this now and see what he's got."

"It still only comes out to a 45."

"The moron! We should be afraid to send this kid out into the world for fear he'll hurt himself." Laughter. "How many more do I have to change?"

"Six. I think he needs six more right."

"Six? How is that possible? He can't add! The kid's 20 years old and he can't even add. He's not retarded, he's an imbecile!" The laughter escalated.

I moved away from the window so as not to be seen. Inside the room sat the senior math teacher and his paraprofessional. I remembered a conversation I had had with this same teacher regarding teaching strategies early on that year.

"My students have a 90% pass rate. Do you hear what I'm saying? You want to know how I make that happen? I pass out one sheet of the exam each day, and for the whole semester, we review. That's my secret."

Just fresh from a two year teaching stint on Rikers Island, and glad to be on the outside, I faded far from the door. I would never speak about this to anyone.

I'm inside the school psychologist's office on Rikers Island. He is a gay man who often confides in me about the abusive relationship, which he's presently in.

"Jay infuriates me." The psych says. He has opened a small, old style film case and poured its contents out onto his desk. There is a small amount of marijuana and a number of mostly smoked joints. "I hit him sometimes. He just makes me do it."

We're inside a large prison facility in one of the smaller buildings that serves as the high school, and I'm a little nervous that this man now has drugs out on the table.

He sees me staring at him. "I'm counting my roaches. I need to make sure that I have enough of them for two good joints. That's the amount I need to get me to the spot."

I'm still looking at him. "I re-up every Thursday. And…" he's counting. "We're good." He begins to pack them back into his film vial. "I can't imagine what I would do if I ran out. I'd probably go home and crack Jay's skull."

"Let's hope it doesn't come to that."

Pablo, the psychologist, looks directly at me. He awakens into the silence between us. "I imagine this must all look at little odd to you." He says. "I hope you don't judge me."

"No. How could I possibly judge you?"

One day we will help Pablo move out of his boyfriend's house. We will accompany him that day so he won't hurt his lover. The apartment is lovely, and the lover cowers on a leather recliner tucked away in one corner of the wood finished living room. He is hurt that Pablo is leaving, and he is afraid because we are here. I cannot imagine violence in this relationship; all I can see is two lost people hurting for one another.

One of our teachers is a retired firefighter who colors his hair with black shoe polish that he often forgets on the bathroom sink, and another can't close the stall door while he's sitting on the toilet because he's claustrophobic; when you open the bathroom door early in the morning, you are confronted by the image of him smiling at you with his pants down. Why he has to come all the way to the prison each morning to move his bowels is beyond my understanding, but this place is about survival, so I'm not questioning anyone about anything. Not even the art teacher who flew into a rage one morning after she'd discovered that she lost a pair of scissors.

"Goddammit, where are those fucking scissors!" she screamed.
"Relax. They'll turn up."
"Yeah, probably in some kid's back."
"I hadn't thought about that."
"Yeah, well, we work in a prison and everything is a weapon." She paused. "Doctor told me I could have a glass of wine when I come home from work. To relax me. Of course I found the biggest glass in the house. Practically takes the whole bottle to fill it."

Cigarettes and liquor have hardened her features. Life, I imagine, has hardened her, too. She is divorced with no children, looking around 55 though only 45 with 20 plus years of teaching experience -- enough time to create a nervous breakdown in most people. I look around the room, marvelling at all the paint and brushes, the variety of construction paper, pens, inks and colored pencils -- an entire room and closet filled with a vibrant variety of tools and supplies begging to be wielded creatively -- creating the most well-equipped art classroom I will ever see in a public school.

I later will hear rumors of how she cleared out all the supplies from her former school, bringing everything here with her, leaving the incoming art teacher with only loose leaf paper and pencils.

I am the Union Rep. I haven't joined the Union yet, but that doesn't seem to trouble anyone. I have taken the position because no one else wants it. The first thing people do is send me to the principal's office with a list of grievances. Of course, they persuade me to not attach names to any one specific grievance. My conversation with the principal goes something like this:

"Ms. Grey." She looks up and smiles as I stand in her doorway. "I'd like to speak with you about some matters – if you have the time."

"Sure. Why don't you sit down."

I sit across from her desk.

"You know I'm the Union Rep now."

She nods, still trying to smile.

"And some people have come to me and said that we're not working according to contract here."

"Exactly how are we not working in accordance with the contract?"

"Well, for one thing, there are safety issues. Someone suggested that we have a Correction Officer in each room."

"In each room."

"Yes."

"And that's in the contract?"

"Well I never saw it there."

"Go on."

"And the hours. People are saying that we can't be obligated to start at 7:30 in the morning. That this is an issue the entire school should vote on."

"They said that."

"Yes."

"They also mentioned that we're locked in the building. And that it's against Board of Ed policy to lock a classroom door, so locking the entire building leaves us out of compliance with the contract."

"They do realize that we're working in a prison?"

"Well, they say that we're working in a school, not in a prison."

"It's a school inside of a prison."

"Yes."

"A few people suggested that you should exercise your authority with the Department of Corrections to enforce a more traditional school day."

"Exactly who are these people?"

"Well, they didn't really wish to be identified."

"They didn't."

"No. They specifically told me not to mention their names. Just to say that these were "general gripes" from the staff as a whole."

"They told you to say this?"

"They were emphatic about it."

"Well, let me give you some advice. For you. As the Union Rep. The next time some of your esteemed colleagues have a complaint, let them attach their name to it."

"Is that legal?"

"That's procedure."

We sit for a long time in silence.

"They set me up."

She nods her head. I get up, thank her and leave.

As I am leaving, she says, "Be careful what people send you in here to do."

I refused to defend the pedophile who had been caught performing oral sex on a 15 year old inmate -- despite what the District Rep insisted that I do.

"But Anthony, he did it."

"He has rights."

"You're not listening, this guy is guilty."

"He's a professional. We're not going to let any administrator push him around..."

"The fucking guy did it. Will you let this go?"

"He did it?"

"That's what I'm telling you."

"He still has rights."

"That's fine. Let him have his rights someplace else."

There's a silence between us.

"He called me."

"What?"

"He's terrified of losing his livelihood."

"His livelihood? Don't you get it: He's a pedophile in a prison for boys."

"He's a professional."

"He's a liar. When I asked him if he'd done anything wrong, he swore to me that he hadn't. Then, when I tell the guy that he might have to work someplace else -- but that he wouldn't lose his career -- he grabs me, digs his fingernails into my arm and says, 'You don't understand. I don't want another job. I need this job.' The look in this guy's eyes scared me. I still didn't know what he'd done, but I felt dirty after that."

"You're sure he did it? I mean, he sounded pretty sincere to me."

"When the AP walked in on him, he was on his knees blowing the kid."

"The AP saw this."

"From 10 feet away. Clear as day."

"Who told you this?"

"The AP. Off the record."

"You weren't supposed to talk with him."

"He didn't want to, but I pushed him. After the guy grabbed me like that, I needed to know what happened."

"Okay. But we're still going to defend him."

"Fine. Just make sure he never works here again."

I was raw in those days. Once, at a City wide Union meeting, I grew tired of listening to person after person get up in front of the auditorium and tell Alvarado that they didn't want him running for President of the UFT. Alvarado, who instituted the full day kindergarten at a time when there was no pre-k, had been, according to rumor, caught with his hands in the till and then lost his position as Chancellor of the Board of Education after only one year. He was now trying to become President of the Union. So I got up in front of that huge auditorium and said this into the open mic:

"I don't understand why we're still discussing this. This man said that he wouldn't run for Union President if we didn't want him to." I turned to him on stage. "You did say that."

He didn't answer. I repeated it.

He reluctantly shook his head in acknowledgement. "So what's the issue here? I think we've all made it pretty clear that we don't want him." I looked at him again. His head was down. "So why don't we all just go home." Alvarado never ran after that.

"You know, as a teacher I didn't support the Union. It wasn't that I was against what they were trying to do. I just wouldn't go out on strike." The AP from Rikers is speaking with me as I'd just become the Union Rep.

"Why not?"

"Because of the students. We'd worked hard enough to convince them to come to school in the first place. These were kids who had all kinds of things going on in their lives, sometimes horrible things no one should have to face. Now we're going to shut the doors and tell them they have no place to go. I couldn't do it."

"Over 25 years later, people still don't speak to me because I crossed that picket line. Right after I put in my retirement papers, one of my colleagues from back then called me and this is what he said: "'You don't deserve to retire, you fucking traitor. We earned that retirement for you, you piece of shit.'"

I remember as a child the strike that followed the one Melvin had spoken about. It was 1968, and I had no place to go for nearly seven weeks. At first, it had been fun to stay home, but some time in October I really began to feel sick inside that my school was closed. I worried that I'd never go to school again. With no schooling, I might have to go to work in a factory like some kids back in the 1800's had to. I was ten years old. I even pictured myself as a chimney sweep because of my size.

When we finally returned to class, the teachers were bitter because they all had to pay back two days wages for each day they had gone out on strike, and they had to make up all the lost time by working longer days for the remainder of that year. The Taylor Law had been enforced for the first time against city employees.

My fifth grade teacher privately cursed the Union to me: "The Union is supposed to protect us, not make our lives more difficult. It'll be another five years before I can retire now." She shook her head as she hurriedly packed her belongings. I had stayed after class that day to clean the boards. "Look at the time. I'll never catch my train. This is a nightmare." She lived in Long Island and took the LIRR. At that hour she explained the trains were crowded. Each day she arrived home after 6pm exhausted, only to have to make it back to work by seven the next morning. "I'm 65 years old, been teaching for almost 40 years, and this stupid strike has nearly ruined me."

In my twenty fifth year, I worked for a school with four sites, coordinating the registration and grade entry for 1200 students. In addition, I provided technical support to office staff and sometimes to classroom teachers. My job required that I visit each of the locations, which existed in three of the five boroughs whenever I believed it necessary. The staff didn't fully trust me as they thought I was a part of administration, but it didn't stop me from asking people what they thought of their school or their bosses.

Problems began at one of the sites when a young, attractive, female teacher, newly graduated from NYU, was suspected of having an inappropriate relationship with a male student. The teacher appeared stunningly beautiful. I first noticed her bending over a desk in the main office. She seemed to be filling out a form. Fifteen minutes passed and she was still filling out that form, her hourglass figure silhouetted in the contrast of sun, shadow, and fluorescent light.

The Center Administrator refused to report this teacher to the Principal without any substantive evidence. It seemed unlikely that a highly educated and recently married woman would be having sex with a 20 year old inner city youth. And the CA said she would not destroy this woman's career over rumor. The staff, despite this refusal on the CA's part, continued to profess undying love and loyalty toward their leader, yet at the same time relentlessly pursued these allegations against the new teacher by presenting an increasing amount of circumstantial evidence.

An accusation of inappropriate behavior with a student, especially the suggestion that you, as a professional, had engaged in a sexual relationship with one your students, generally marked the end of your career -- even if you hadn't done anything. If you managed to survive that kind of scandal, people remembered the accusation, not the outcome, and treated you accordingly.

The CA's decision to not report what essentially remained rumor seemed prudent. Months later when evidence was uncovered suggesting the teacher's intimate involvement with that student, the CA immediately reported her findings to the Principal, who, in turn, formally notified the DOE. The CA was removed pending an investigation, with the possibility of dismissal and loss of pension on the table because she hadn't immediately reported the earlier rumors to officials at the Department of Education.

This action on the part of the Department of Education stood in stark contrast to how things had been handled 20 plus years before. When I worked in Bushwick, I witnessed the investigation of a young, male teacher who had been accused of inappropriate behavior with female students.

At the time, our students were 17 to 22 years of age; the teacher being investigated was 25, married for several years with two young children. He dressed well, had exceptionally good manners, and always treated women gallantly in my presence.

I watched for days as female students got pulled from classes and ushered into a room where they were questioned about this teacher. Some of the girls being questioned I had encountered in awkward moments. One girl had come up to the front of my classroom to ask me a question and then closed quarters on me, causing me to back up repeatedly or face the prospect of having her breasts pressed against me. At one point, I actually tripped backwards over the trashcan and everyone laughed.

I reported the incident to the principal who told me that I had to make allowances for things like this as she was "simply trying out her new and considerable equipment." Another of the girls had come up during homeroom and placed her crotch over the corner of the desk, and while she spoke with me, appeared to slowly fuck the desk. After she'd left the room, two other girls spoke to me about the incident: "We saw what she did." one said.

The other said, "We have your back." Their responses confirmed that I hadn't imagined the whole thing, which seemed beyond belief at the time.

I'd encountered a third of these girls alone in the room with a male student. She'd been speaking as I entered, and the male student had been seated with his mouth open, the two of them held in this moment where she spoke rapidly, her body pushing forward, her arms partially squeezed together in a manner that had caused her breasts to overflow from her blouse, and the young man sat unable to move, perhaps unable to even hear anything she'd been saying. I idiotically reprimanded her for allowing herself to be alone in a room with a male student while behaving in a suggestive manner. In turn, my colleagues had reprimanded me for acting like her father.

After their investigation had concluded, they fired the teacher, and then I found out that over the past two years, he'd been warned several times by his colleagues about his behavior. Apparently, he had a giant penis and it had somehow unhinged him into believing that every girl wanted to be speared open by him. He'd whispered things like, "Oh baby, I could please you deeply and fully in ways you've never been pleased," in the ears of girls while he walked around his class supposedly helping them with their math. He went as far as to describe his prodigious penis, in an effort to convince them to have sex with him. Some of these girls were amused by his insanity; others felt horrified, disgusted, and fouly violated.

So for two prior years, he'd been warned, first informally and then formally, that if he continued, they'd have to have him fired. Each time he'd promised to stop but always picked up again shortly afterwards. While he hadn't actually slept with any of the girls as they all found him creepy, he would sometimes put his hands on their shoulders while he whispered disgusting things in their ears.
So when they removed the CA instantly for refusing to report the possibility that this 23 year old female teacher may be having consensual sex with a 20 year male student -- inappropriate as such a relationship would have been -- it seemed harsh.

Something interesting happened after the CA had been removed. The staff, who openly admitted during the DOE's investigation that they'd brought this matter to the CA's attention on many occasions and felt frustrated when she had refused to act on it -- their testimonies ending up being the damning evidence against their beloved CA -- then blamed the Principal, who had reported the incident to the Department of Education's investigative unit, for the CA's removal. In retribution, the staff unionized, refusing to run the school outside of union contract, which in effect, shut down education in that building. The success of the school had been predicated on the staff's ability to work outside of the box and the contract. Next, the staff at the Lower Manhattan site ran the first replacement Center Administrator out of the building within a month. They took two months to run the second AP out.

During that time, I shared an office with an old timer named Will, a jazz musician who had formerly dated Aretha Franklin's sister. Will worked as the school's messenger, so people who didn't know his background saw him as a harmless old man who picked up and delivered the mail. People hardly noticed him. At 70, he still travelled on tour to Europe to play jazz, but in our school, most people just saw him as old Will. We had this conversation one day.

"Man, you just won't believe what's going on in the downtown site."

"What's wrong?"

"That whole staff has gone crazy. They just about ruined that school."

"They keep filing grievances against the Principal." I said.

"That ain't the half of it. I heard a teacher telling her students the other day that they shouldn't bother coming to this school because it ain't no good anymore. And then this thing with Kelvin." Kelvin was the newest AP.

"What happened with Kelvin?"

"They took him out in an ambulance."

"He okay?"

"I don't know. But what got me was Kelvin had collapsed in the office and no one, I mean no one did anything. Staff members kept on working. People came into the office, saw him lying on the floor, and just went about their business. Only Olivia called 911 and tried to help him. And now the staff hates her. I never seen such cold heartedness"

There were a ridiculous number of grievances filed against the principal that year. I spoke with one of the investigators who'd been coming into the building almost weekly. He'd taken to hanging out in my office until the principal arrived as I was there early and my AC worked.

"Man, you here again?"

He laughed. "Yeah."

"So what is it this time?"

"Does it really matter? When a school gets this many grievances, it's one of two things: either everything is wrong with the place, which doesn't seem to be the case here, or somebody's got a grudge against the principal."

"Multiple people." He laughed again. "So if you know it's disgruntled individuals trying to make trouble for the principal, what do you do?"

"We show up, spend half an hour here, and then leave."

"You don't investigate?"

"Not after 45 grievances in one year, especially after the first 30 proved groundless."

"So why is this permitted to go on? The principal's got an ulcer over this shit"

"I'm not surprised, but there's nothing anyone can do. We have to show up. In the end, it's the school that suffers. People poison everything when they're filled with this kind of hate. It's like they're burning the building down, yelling, 'Fire! Fire!' Only they're splashing gasoline on everything."

More than half the staff of the Lower Manhattan site quit that year. There had been rumors that the former CA had orchestrated the entire Lower Manhattan failed coup from her new position down at the District Office in an attempt to get even with the Principal, whom she blamed for everything. And while the CA had been seen on several occasions meeting with key agitators from Lower, it all just remained rumor.

~

I sat in darkness, examining the people around me through the mirror behind the bar as I no longer could look another person in the eye. "Look at that loser." I thought to myself, letting a laugh escape.

"He's pathetic." When I saw the image in the mirror laugh, I felt shock and horror that I had been looking at myself: I had grown fat and my face looked bloated and sad.

I only wanted to drink, get high, and disappear into the darkness of a topless bar where I silently watched the form of a beautiful woman moving to the rhythms of my own discontent.

Chapter Three

The Check is in the Mail

It's possible to ignore how dysfunctional you are when engaged by a bureaucracy that is both comically and tragically more dysfunctional than you may ever become. It's like going to the movies to escape, to watch someone else struggle through the fantastically unimaginable, and while you hope they come out on top as they often do, you're entertained and relieved in the end because that nonsense isn't yours. In effect, you forget the tragedy of your own sadly comedic existence.

~

When I first started working for the New York City Board of Education as it was called back then, the bureaucracy frightened most people. I had spent a couple of years in the military so I felt familiar with endless paperwork, being sent from one department to another only to be sent back again, with little to show for it.

In the military, they had an expression, "Hurry up and wait." And every time you tried to get something done, people told you this as an explanation for why you might be endlessly ushered about in order to get something seemingly simple done.

Those Who Can't

As Sgt Shotwell, my Flight Chief, once said in his sardonic southern drawl, "There's your way, there's my way, there's the right way, there's the wrong way, and then there's the military way. Son, we're in the military, so none of those other ways matter."

Bureaucracy became inculcated into your being within months of being in the service. One night while I worked the graveyard shift as a new police officer, I heard this call come across the radio at around 1:00 am: "Base police to police four, report to the hospital to pick up one perambulator."

I asked my partner on the Main Gate what a perambulator was and he told me that it didn't matter, that they were just messing with the new guy. I still didn't understand.

"It's a quiet night on base. The flight chief is bored so he's going to send Simpson, who's driving Police Four on his own tonight, to the hospital to pick up a perambulator, which happens to be a baby carriage -- only no one will know what he's talking about and they'll probably just throw him out."

I immediately got into the spirit of the thing, picked up the phone and called the hospital. I explained the situation to the Sgt on duty and told him to tell Simpson that he can't pick up the perambulator without a perambulator request form. In a heartbeat, the guy on the other end was all in.

A few moments later, this call came across the radio. "Police four to base police. Can't pick up the perambulator without the proper forms."

The Desk Sgt got involved now, creating a perambulator request form. The Flight Chief acted irate at not getting what he wanted right away, cursing the military for its bureaucracy.

An hour later, Simpson has gone back and forth to the hospital twice: once for the perambulator request form and a second time to return with the perambulator release form properly authorized -- the result of a conspiracy between the Desk Sgt, the Flight Chief and the Sgt at the hospital. In the end, Simpson returned to the station with a funnel attached to a rubber hose -- an original creation courtesy of our man at the hospital.

"Hey, Sarge," Simpson said. "So how's this thing work?"

The Flight Chief had Simpson put the rubber hose to his ear and then he spoke through the funnel, "You fucking dummy!"

That was the military. No surprises. Even Simpson laughed. The Board of Education with its endless paperwork and bureaucratic mazery stood as a whole different sort of beast. If you ever tried to phone someone down at 65 Court Street for help, after being redirected through several phone calls you'd inevitably find yourself speaking with the original person who had picked up the phone -- only now this person had grown less than patient with you because of your stupidity.

"I thought I told you to call Cheryl at 2844? Why didn't you do what I told you to do?"

"I did call Cheryl, only she's not at 2844."

"So then why you calling me?"

"She told me to call Dan. Dan had no idea what any of this was about and suggested I call Francine. Francine assured me that Mr. Williams handles this sort of thing. Mr. Williams, who seems rather old (she laughed at this) doesn't handle anything to do with teachers. He suggested that I call you."

"Okay. Let me see. Oh, try calling Mrs. Lee."

Five phone calls later. "Yes it's me again."

"I've already told you that I don't handle this. Did you call Mrs. Lee?"

"Yes. And…"

"I don't want to hear the whole story."

"But she assured me that this was your department…"

"How did you get my number anyway? You need to stop calling me. What about 'I don't handle this' don't you understand?"

"Well then, who does handle it?"

"How would I know?"

"People keep directing me back to you."

"Who the hell keeps telling you to call me? You need to stop listening to those people."

Before I began teaching, I had the rare experience of actually working at 65 Court Street one summer for the Auditor General's Office. I'd done temp work for the Board, checking the attendance books at different schools to see if people were taking attendance properly, which they weren't at any of the 25 schools we'd visited. Then I'd been placed inside the Office of Auditor General for the months of June and July.

For the first two weeks inside the Board, I worked very hard in this huge room full of largely empty desks, rarely looking up to catch my breath. When I did come up for air, I noticed this one man had appeared at a desk in the middle of the room. No one else sat around him.

For whatever reason, he caught my attention, and I became fascinated with him over the next few weeks. What I noticed was how he simply didn't seem to be doing anything. Occasionally, he'd pick his nose. Otherwise, he just sat completely still at a desk with a phone that never rang. Never once did I see him making a phone call. He never wrote anything, read anything or spoke to anyone. For three weeks I watched him, more and more each day, and then he simply disappeared.

That got me interested in what other people were doing on the floor. By then, I knew who did payroll because she always went on about how difficult it was. There was a lot of movement in the office, and pockets of conversation flared up here and there. It seemed that people were working hard and constantly, with few breaks.

When I looked closer, I noticed that at around 9:00 am a group of people gathered around the coffee machine. And again at 10:15, which was time for the 15 minute break guaranteed by contract. At noon, the floor became a ghost town. And then at 2:45, the second 15 minutes break, people congregated around the snack table, and everyone was packed up and ready to leave by 4:45, waiting in conversation with their belongings by the time clock to punch out at 5:00 pm.

I watched more closely, this time passing by the little groups. I saw that there was an ebb and flow of movement in this office, with people gathering at different places throughout the day. What I never saw was anyone working. The payroll woman complained all week and then into the next about having to do payroll. She spent the better parts of two weeks going on about it, but she never did anything. She'd spend a few hours knocking out payroll twice a month, and the rest of the time she engaged in personal conversations around the office, called her friends and family on the phone or took water breaks, coffee breaks, bathroom breaks or smoke breaks.

Every once in a while, an argument of sorts would break out. It almost inevitably erupted around someone being asked to do something by someone else.

"I'm not doing that. That's not in my job description. I don't know who he think he is." These eruptions allowed the disgruntled person to spend time visiting colleagues in order to vent.

"Oh yeah, I remember when he asked me to do that very same thing. Uh-uh. I got my hands full as it is. You have to draw the line or they'll work you to death."

I came to the conclusion that no one in that office worked. Instead, they had cleverly developed a series of routines that gave the appearance they worked but nothing got done -- except their own payroll. That always got taken care of.

So when I called the DOE as a teacher, it didn't surprise me that no one wanted to do anything. Phone calls were a nuisance to the people who picked up the phones and a waste of time to anyone making them. The only solution was to visit in person.

Payroll and anything connected with salary increases required your presence. You might as well simply stop a stranger on the street and ask him for help as call someone down there. And the way people refused you, you'd think they were giving up their own money.

My first experience with payroll was as a new teacher on Rikers Island. Someone kind had taken me under his wing and actually sat down with me, insisting that I fill out all the paperwork that had been laid out before me. It looked endless, even with my military background, and it took hours to finish. Back then, each department had its own forms where information was duplicated. Payroll, personnel, and health benefits required three different sets of forms. When my kind friend saw that I had become discouraged, he spoke to me most confidentially.

"You need to finish the paperwork if you ever want to get paid."

That caught my attention. "What do you mean by 'ever want to get paid'? Exactly how long will I have to wait until I get paid?"

"That's a good question."

"Okay."

"You see that guy over there." He nodded toward one of my colleagues who looked particularly disgruntled, as if a dark cloud loomed over him at all times. I had specifically avoided ever speaking to this man because of his foul demeanor. "He hasn't been paid in eight months."

"You're kidding. How could that be?"

"He didn't fill out his paperwork properly."

Payroll wasn't responsible for anything. That's how they operated. Perhaps the entire Board of Education -- at least the bureaucratic side of it anyhow -- couldn't be held accountable: If something went wrong, something failed to get done, it always rested on someone else's shoulders -- some vague and unknown person -- or it was your own fault, even if it wasn't, and people would go to great lengths to point this out to you.

"Well, didn't you fill out the W3F405?"

"No."

"Well that explains it."

"No one gave me that form."

"Well that's not our fault, is it?"

"How was I supposed to know?"

"Look, you want to get paid, right?"

"Yes."

"Well try filling out the paperwork properly!"

Often, the school's payroll secretary would tell you that you had to go down to 65 Court Street yourself or you'd never get paid. Back then, you could actually take the elevator up to the 8th floor and get off, ask to speak with a payroll advisor and then sit with an individual -- only it almost never went well.

I recall sitting face to face with a payroll specialist in a small cubicle as it became abundantly clear that this individual assigned to help me had no clue what he was doing. Before I could say anything, providence intervened.

We were in a room filled with cubicles where a dozen people were consulting payroll specialists like the one who sat in front of me. I heard voices rising and then yelling.

"I'VE BEEN COMING HERE FOR SIX MONTHS. DO YOU HEAR ME? SIX MONTHS! AND NOTHING, I'M TELLING YOU NOTHING HAS BEEN DONE! ARE YOU EVER GOING TO PAY ME?"

"Sir, you have to stop screaming or I'll call security."

More screaming. Objects crashed. We heard security called, the muffled voices followed by rapid footsteps and then the poor man dragged out screaming, "I'LL GET A LAWYER. I SWEAR I'LL GET A LAWYER!"

The payroll advisor and I looked at each other. I remained convivial -- for all five of the trips that I had to make in order to straighten out a minor problem, each time being told that the problem was something the other person had missed.

Eventually, someone lost his mind with a payroll specialist, choked the person and then threatened to kill himself by jumping out the window -- only all windows were permanently sealed, so you can imagine how that worked out for the guy. After that, they closed the floor to anyone but payroll specialists. The DOE made the area high security, so you couldn't even get off the elevator on the 8th floor any longer. This worked just fine for the payroll specialists who never answered the phone.

Once I did call with an issue, and someone actually picked up the phone. After a while of his being rather helpful, he told me that he was new.

"I know. You answered the phone."

Several calls later, he confided in me that his supervisor had told him that he couldn't speak to me any longer about my issue. He would, however, try to straighten it out, but if it didn't get fixed that I was not to call him any more. He simply wouldn't be allowed to speak with me.

Salary Differentials was another monster. You went to this department to get increases in salary based on educational requirements you had met. As a teacher, you were required to get a Masters' Degree to keep your position, and you had to document it a second time in order to receive the related pay increase.

If you failed to get your Master's degree within five years of being appointed, the personnel department would simply terminate you. Even if personnel approved your Master's Degree for the purposes of employment retention, the salary differential department insisted on its own separate set of paperwork, including official transcripts.

Official transcripts is where they got you. Back then, no one, and I mean no one, could get hold of an official transcript. The only option open to anyone was to have the University send a sealed official transcript directly to the Board of Education. And they never seemed to receive them. No matter how many you sent.

On my second visit to salary differentials, which had most of its own floor, they informed me that my transcripts still hadn't arrived. I told them that I had had the college send a second set. And I had been assured that these were sent.

"Then you should check with records."

Records was yet another floor. So I went to records. There seemed to be a lot of people working in records. I had to fill out a form to request my records. An hour later I was told that they couldn't find any records.

"What do you mean you can't find any records?"

"Just what I said. You ain't got no records."

"How's that possible?"

"How should I know. I just work here."

We looked at each other. Then this woman said something amazing to me. "You want to check for yourself?"

"Sure." Is all I could say.

In the back of records, amongst all the filing cabinets, I realized that the multitude of people who appeared to be working in records were like me: people off the street wandering through the personnel files of the entire Board of Education *completely unsupervised!*

I found my file. Inside of my nearly empty folder, which had been misfiled, I discovered a cover sheet stamped with time and date, stating that they had received and accepted my transcripts. I returned to the front desk with the evidence in hand.

"You received my transcripts, only you lost them."

"I didn't lose anything."

"Somebody did."

"Well, you need to send us another copy."

"I already sent you two copies. I'm not sending you a third. And I'm keeping this as evidence of your incompetence."

"No you're not. SECURITY!"

I was able to flee the building down a side staircase with page in hand. I found myself so livid over the experience that I couldn't sleep. Eventually, I decided that I would request a third set of official transcripts. I had tried showing up with student transcripts but was told that "only official transcripts could be accepted." I had even explained the situation and shown the evidence of their malfeasance, but I was told "Sorry, we can't help you."

While requesting the new transcripts, which were to be sent to the Board of Education, 65 Court Street, I got a brilliant idea. I requested a second set of official transcripts to be sent to the Cuban Institute of Higher Learning at 166 Court Street. I happened to live at 166 Court Street at the time with my Cuban wife. I figured no one would check if there were actually a Cuban Institute of Higher Learning. And they didn't.

When I appeared at salary differentials this time, they told me yet again that my transcripts still hadn't arrived. They made me go down to records and this time I wasn't allowed to check my own file, but no, there were no transcripts.

Then I returned to Salary Differentials and produced my official transcripts.

"Where did you get these?"

"It doesn't matter."

"You're not supposed to have these."

"I do."

"These are official transcripts."

"Yes, I know." I took a breath. "You can look at them. You can even make copies of them, but you can't keep them."

"I don't know if that's going to work."

"I've sent you three copies of my official transcripts and you've lost all three copies. I even have this piece of paper showing that you actually received my second set."

"Let me see that. Where did you get this?"

"From my file."

"You're not supposed to take anything out of my file."

"It's evidence that you've lost my transcripts. So here is a set for you to use. I want them back."

I must have looked like a crazy person. The woman made copies, made notations, had me sign a few things and then handed back my official transcripts. Nine months later, I received my differential.

As a teacher, you had two separate payrolls: regular and per session. Per session monies were earned by working additional jobs beyond the scope of your teaching day: after school, night school, and summer school. In other professions, they call that overtime, and you're paid time and a half. A teacher working overtime received a flat rate, which amounted to about half the wage of a top salaried teacher.

Teachers were paid by the payroll secretary on payday after the checks got delivered to the school. Checks almost always arrived late, but they arrived. Per session checks were mailed to your house. And sometimes they never got there. Once I received a phone call from a complete stranger who asked me to identify myself, was I a teacher, she wanted to know. I told her, "Yes, what is this about?" She said that she lived in the neighborhood and was holding my per session check. That it had been stuck to the back of hers. So I walked over to her house, showed her my official ID and picked up my check.

Another time, my check simply never arrived. After three weeks of waiting and several phone calls to the Board of Ed, I was told, "Your check is in the mail." On the Board's advice, I had a stop payment ordered and the check reissued. Several weeks later a check arrived -- only it was the first check.

"You can't cash that."

"Why?"

"Because you had us issue a stop payment on it."

"Can't you unstop the stop?"

"No. A new check has already been issued."

"I'll return that one. If it ever arrives."

"If you try to cash this check, you could go to jail."

"Jesus Christ, it took six weeks for the check to get here. I live 11 blocks from the Board. You could have strapped it on the back of a turtle and it would have gotten here faster."

"It's your own fault for insisting that we issue a stop payment."

"You suggested that I do that. It took 42 days for the check to arrive. You don't think that that's a little excessive?"

"That's the Postal Service, not us."

The new check arrived three months later. And I was glad to get it.

You'd imagine that after 27 years, all of this would have changed. And it had. Sort of.

When I retired, I found myself looking at a full paycheck two weeks after they should have stopped paying me. Three months before, I discovered that I no longer had health care -- at least according to what was now called the New York City Department of Education.

The problem all began when I went in for my retirement consultation. The UFT (our union) has a retirement consultation, which they strongly recommended you attend, and the Teacher's Retirement System has its own consultation. Everyone attends both. Unfortunately, you're told different things at each of them, and while about half of what the Union tells you is true and most of what TRS tells you is true, they provide you with contradictory information. In the end, you have no idea what's true and what's not until it's too late.

After the UFT consultation, I ended up rushing down to the DOE to straighten out my healthcare for fear that if I didn't do so *immediately*, I'd end up paying $14,000 a year out of my pocket for healthcare after retirement-- something the Union had insisted would happen if I didn't act immediately.

"You don't have health care." The woman behind her computer said to me, glancing over to make sure I had heard her.

"What?"

"According to my records, not only don't you have health care, but you've never had health care of any sort with the City of New York. You simply don't exist."

"I've worked for 27 years. How's that possible?"

"I don't know. I can only tell you what I see here." And then. "When's the last time you went to the doctor?"

"Two months ago."

"And you had health care then?"

"Yes. My whole family has my health care."

"Well I don't show any record of that."

I found out in this woman's office that upon retirement I could elect to sign up with any health care provider whom I wished. There had been no rush.

"Since you have no health care, you should probably sign up for something."

So I signed up for Emblem, which cost nothing in retirement.

"What about CIGNA?"

"What about CIGNA?"

"I still have it."

"Not according to the DOE you don't."

"Yeah, but I know I have it. Can't you cancel it for me?"

"How can I cancel it when our records don't indicate you even have it?"

"So, I'm going to have two kinds of health care."

"That's illegal."

"What do I do?"

"Wait for the Emblem to go through. When you get the ID cards, you call CIGNA and explain to them what's going on and tell them to cancel it for you." She saw the distressed look on my face. "Look, there's no way the City is going to let you get away with having two health care providers."

When I called CIGNA a month and a half later, they told me that I couldn't cancel the policy -- that only the City of New York could, that the City was CIGNA's client, not me. I called the DOE, and they suggested that I wait until I retire as the insurance would be cancelled automatically.

At the end of February, a full month after my retirement date, I found myself with another paycheck which I wasn't supposed to get -- only now they were deducting huge amounts to pay for the CIGNA coverage they claimed I no longer had.

It's only then that I realized I felt terrified of the DOE and its constituents.

Two years before, when I had decided to plan for an early retirement, I began doing the numbers. Then I got a letter in the mail from the TRS stating that they had done some recalculating, and I owed them nearly $13,000 in back contributions to my retirement plan. For a variety of reasons, payroll had simply stopped automatically deducting money for short periods of time throughout my career. Over 25 years, the amount not deducted had grown to quite a sum. And this, they pointed out, had been my fault.

A month and a half after I retired -- not during the retirement consultation where I repeatedly asked TRS, "Is there anything else I should know" -- I was informed that they could not even begin to process my retirement until I paid back the remaining $8,000.

"When were you going to tell me this?"

"You should have known this."

In late February after my retirement, I called Human Resources at the DOE to straighten out the health care issue. The average wait time on the phone is one hour. Sometimes they accidentally hung up on you. I told the young man the story about CIGNA and he told me that it's illegal for me to have two healthcare providers.

We danced a little.

At first, he told me that I didn't have CIGNA, but some extensive research on his part got this response, "You do have CIGNA! And Emblem!"

"I told you.

"This isn't good."

The Check is in the Mail

"I know. That's why I'm calling you."

"You don't understand. These people are going to come after you."

"Come after me? I didn't do anything."

"And you think that matters? You know how these people are. They'll hold you responsible and want their money back."

It was true and I knew it.

"So do something."

Another hour later, he assured me that I no longer had CIGNA. Three months later, when I finally got paid for the extra work I continued to do for my school after I had retired, I discovered that they were still deducting CIGNA from my checks.

Each phone call to HR retirement required that I wait at least one hour on hold. After several calls to a Mrs. Patters, I was again assured that CIGNA had been cancelled and no more money would be deducted.

"What about the $1700 they mistakenly deducted after I retired?"

That took most of a year to get back. And many phone calls. My favorite was the one that went like this:

"You still didn't get that money back?"

"No."

"I thought we took care of that?"

"Me too."

"Let me ask around."

When Mrs Patters got back to me, she told me this: "These people around here all have amnesia. We goin' to have to do this all over again."

This time I ended up, on her recommendation, first contacting her supervisor and then writing a letter directly to the head of health care services for the City of New York. And following it up with a phone call that went something like this:

"I don't know what you're talking about. You sure you got the right number?"

I had just finished telling my story. Then I mentioned the letter I had sent and the woman's name to whom I had sent it.

Silence. "Oh, why didn't you say so. She's the new head of the department. I'll look right into that."

Right after retirement, I couldn't get off payroll. I literally begged people to stop paying me, but all I got was, "It's not my job. You have to call that other number I gave you."

"But I did call that number and they specifically told me that it was your job."

Well, I don't know what to tell you."

In the end, it was the emails that got the results. No one wants a paper trail. The original person I had called told me confidentially that she hadn't understood that it was her job, and now she would be able to take care of it, only please don't send any more emails -- especially those ccing her bosses.

~

In the end, there is the conviction that everything can be taken away from you, as it sometimes is, and there's nothing you can do about it. Nothing you do, have done, no work you produced, no number of sacrifices you may have made -- none of this matters in the face of bureaucracy. The system and its rules, the people who work it with frightening degrees of contempt and incompetency -- they themselves, having been driven out of their minds by petty micromanagement, by having their humanity repeatedly dashed against the sheer futility of endless and meaningless tasks -- become a beast that devours the human spirit.

Chapter Four

Reputation vs. Experience

J uly has become August and you've begun counting the days to your return; throughout each day a sickening feeling in your stomach intensifies. Your breath shortens, your arm tightens, and then it's three weeks of start up, of days that drown you in endless activity, in planning and execution, in paperwork and organization; trying to place 100 names to as many faces so that you can call order; trying to answer questions from voices that surround you, hopeful eyes that stop you in hallways or find their way into your office -- only to be interrupted by colleagues whose questions take you to other places, and now you're late for another class, for advisory, for a meeting with a parent. You pick up your coffee as the phone rings.

    There are no breaks in these days, only moments when you can sip that coffee or take a mouthful of food or simply exhale, only to be interrupted by something unexpected, something left undone, someone who has just one more question. Days end and you spend hours alone finishing up, but sometimes you're just too tired so you come home to collapse on the couch, awakening in darkness to plan and fortify. And then it begins again. You crawl towards your first day off, towards that weekend when maybe you can get a hold of this thing.

It's October, things are moving, but the class thins out days before Halloween, and again around Thanksgiving -- only a number of your students don't return this time until after Christmas break. You call, email, text them; you ask their friends what's happened to them; the office staff has done the same. And then they're back: sometimes they share the real reason; sometimes they just look at you, remembering nothing -- only within weeks they are expected to be prepared for state exams.

In the last two and a half weeks of January, one semester ends and another begins. Exams are marked, grades are entered; you collect materials and set curriculum in place to teach again, while students come and go, wanting to know why they didn't pass, why they won't graduate until next January or June.

Then you're teaching again, new classes where you have to establish a routine and rhythm only to have it broken in three weeks by an oddly placed winter recess: having to push that rock back up the hill a second time just as you had almost gotten it moving under its own momentum.

There's March, that long, cold month with no days off, followed by a Spring Break where you return to an eight week run through May and into the June madness with students begging for extensions as grades are entered, state exams are marked, and graduation takes place or doesn't for some -- all of which requires at least a full week or two of your July to recover from. Then it's August and you're counting days again.

No matter how much you do, something's always left undone. There's every Sunday night during the school year when you can't sleep thinking about returning to the classroom on Monday, when sometimes the anxiety gets hold of you and you wonder privately if you can go on, but you get up each day and endure. Some days are good where you are moved by the beauty of it all; other days you feel war-worn. The last day of each June you pile all the chairs on desks and push them into a single corner of your now barren room. You take one last look then close that door.

Once you stop, leave the classroom for good, the relief is magical and almost instantaneous; you think to yourself, "Why did I ever put myself through that?" no matter how much you loved teaching, the students, the calling. And you may miss it, but you really rather not go back as it simply takes too much from a person.

You use your heart and soul to speak to the lost ones; you struggle to open that door, to let some light shine in with the hope it will turn some of them around, always aware of how quickly that door can slam shut again. You suffer with them or grow angry at them or at how helpless you feel when you are unable to make a difference. Some fall. Maybe you'll never find out if they ever get back up. You miss the ones that succeed but feel glad they're gone. No matter how much you do, it is never enough. That has been teaching for me: a steady draining and filling of my heart.

~

One of the most difficult things about teaching, about interacting with 100 plus different personalities whose names you have to remember, whose work you have to read, whose lives you need to know something about, is classroom management. How do you manage room after room of 30 plus teenagers who'd rather be texting, chatting, sexting, smoking, drinking, surfing the net, posting, tweeting, facebooking, instagramming, youtubing, vining, snapchatting, acting out on personal drama, having sex -- anything other than spending time with you?

All teachers set rules. Those rules, when consistent with a community and representative of realistic expectations that most students can regularly meet or over time learn to meet, work. The trick is to be consistent and even handed as their teacher. It isn't personal -- even when it is. And it does get deeply personal, only you, as the adult, are required to separate yourself.

I was once told by a trained therapist that a particular person who continuously behaved in an abusive manner toward me was "projecting."

"It isn't personal. It isn't even about you."

"But she's yelling at me, about me. It sure feels personal."

And that's the dilemma: teenagers are continuously acting out on their own issues without even knowing it, and hormonally they are often times unreasonably, perhaps even insanely unbalanced, and you, as the teacher -- as well as other students in the room -- become the likely target. What do you do?

One of the most powerful tools is your reputation with your students. That reputation and the relationship which ensues because of it can be established in a moment or over time, but it is most effectively passed down through community interactions, by what students say about you and how they behave towards you, and this is reinforced by consistency on your part.

I remember getting back into the classroom after a five year break; those five years I'd spent managing the school's data, overseeing a number of online systems, and troubleshooting the school's technology, including programming servers, networking, and maintaining multiple computer labs. Now I found myself teaching again -- something that I thought I'd never again do: I had made my peace with the fact that I'd eventually retire outside of the classroom.

My new class looked and felt chaotic. *I felt uncomfortable.* Students seemed desperate to leave and pained at having to endure me. In their eyes, I wasn't even a real teacher, simply the computer guy with whom they'd gotten stuck. That was who they knew me as. These were young men and women who had grown accustomed to being marginalized, felt some shame over their own struggles in multiple other high schools and in hidden places in their lives, and they finally end up here, a last chance for many of them. Now, not to be even given a "real" teacher was just an affirmation of their own worthlessness.

A colleague of mine, Monique, who had been out of the classroom at one point for three years, bailed me out. She came into my room one afternoon, and I told her that I felt like quitting.

"Naahhh, man, you can't do that."

"Why not? The kids hate me. I can't control the class. I don't know how to teach anymore."

"It'll come back. You just have to hang in there."

"It's not coming back. Kids are transferring out of my class left and right. I never had that happen in my entire life."

"Yeah. I know. One of my advisees wants out of your room.

"What did you tell him?"

"I told him you was cool, to give you a chance. He said the class was complete chaos."

"It probably is."

"I was out of the classroom for three years. When I got back in, I had to stop talking."

"What do you mean?"

"Just what I said: I stopped talking. I mean, I couldn't say shit to them at one point. I simply gave out the work, nodded and kept going. They'd ask me questions, but I ignored them. It was about survival. They even reported me to my supervisor. He'd come in and ask me, 'How you doing?' and I'd just nod at him. By the end of the semester, I was good. The next year, things were smooth again. It was all about getting over that hump. You don't forget. Trust me."

It seemed harsh, to shut down in a classroom on your students, but I had to earn a living. I had young children, and after 23 years in the system, there really were no other options for me. So I trusted Monique and ignored a lot.

One of my worst students frequently left the room and simply disappeared for a good part of the class. As he was abrupt and often disrespectful, I felt glad he was gone. One day the principal came in with this student in tow.

"I found Devon sitting in the stairwell. He says he doesn't feel well. Did you give him permission to leave the room?"

"He told me that he wasn't feeling well. I sent him out to get some air." I lied.

"He doesn't have a pass."

"Sorry, Grayson. How's he doing now?"

"He seems better." He knew I was lying.

After the principal left, I confronted the student,

"Why didn't you tell me you weren't feeling good?"

"Why? What would you have done?" He yelled this at me.

"I would have been able to cover for you. Instead, you made us both look bad." I yelled this back at the student. And then, "You look terrible."

"I got a headache."

"You always got a headache."

"Yeah, well I got things on my mind."

"What things?"

"Personal things."

"Okay. Try writing about them in that journal of yours. Last time I checked, it was nearly blank." He looked at me as if I were being ridiculous. "And leaving the room is out of the question."

"Why?"

"Use your sense, man. You get caught again and where are we then? You need to go to the nurse."

"This school has a nurse?"

"Hell no." Everyone laughed including him. "You can put your head down or sit in the back, whatever will help."

I had students keep daily journals. I encouraged them to come clean in these journals, told them I'd never reveal what was in them or correct them in any way -- unless they were threatening to hurt themselves or another. It was a complete and honest freewrite. One day Devon wrote this:

"My girl is pregnant and I don't even have a job. I got no money, no place for us to live and I can't seem to finish school. I'm 19 years old and I don't want to start dealing drugs again as I'm still on parole."

"No wonder you got a headache all the time." I said to him. He looked at me. "I read your journal."

"Yeah, well, that's confidential."

"You got it. Maybe we can work on getting you out of here." When he looked concerned, I added, "By getting you to graduate."

"Oh."

Students shared their journals in class. Some of them were deeply personal. One of the girls who was only 16 wrote this:

"When you're young, there's the idea that the world will adjust to help you get by. As a teenager, when you have a life changing experience, the way you see things will be altered for the rest of your life. When I was sixteen, which I still am, my life changed forever. I found out that some innocent person would have to depend on me for the rest of her life, and the life I had lived would never be the same.

On March 03, 2013 my daughter, Mercedes Alana Sanchez, was born. I believed that my mother would help me out forever, but now I was a mother. During the process of being pregnant, I was alone. The only person who was there for me was my boyfriend. I hated being in my house with people looking down on me, judging for getting pregnant at such a young age."

"You got a kid?" One young man said after she'd read this entry aloud.

"Yes."

"I would have never known." A girl said.

"You look so young."

Up until that point, she had been some young, pretty, innocent who couldn't possibly understand what the others were going through.

After that, Ivonne had a place of acceptance in the room, was no longer hiding this secret that she felt shame over, and other students felt more comfortable both with her and themselves.

We moved on to the "History of You" essays where more students began to open up. The assignment required that they write a complete history of themselves, focusing on some key moment or event that they believed had shaped their lives. I wanted to set a tone and make the assignment meaningful, so I both helped and encouraged one young lady with a particularly difficult subject. I had her read a draft to the class so that everybody knew what I expected.

"When I was four years old and I couldn't find my other sneaker, my mom got mad in a way I hadn't known before. I don't remember being hit, but I do remember seeing blood on the bathroom door, on my baby brother's crib and on the old times heater. I needed a couple stitches in my head. Thank God I wasn't killed that night or the many other mornings, afternoons or evenings, which followed. From that day on, I carried what had happened with me and lived with the fear that I would be beaten again.

My mom was a strong woman so she really didn't need to use any weapons: Just her mouth, legs and arms. When I say mouth, I mean she would yell at me about what I did wrong or call me names --- anything to bring me down. There were times when I would stay up all night crying because of the pain. I wondered why my mom was always mad or screaming at me. I even thought that life without my mom would be happier. My beatings stopped at the age of seventeen when I was finally brave enough to tell someone I was being abused at home..."

After that, the essays took over the room. One student would sit in a chair in the front and read his essay. The rest of the students would simply listen and then respond. The class was required to ask three questions of the reader. We spent two weeks on this project. One girl wrote this about losing her father to prison:

Thinking back about ten years ago, I was only seven. I had just come back from school. I stepped into my brother's room and I see all my dad's things packed up in a corner. I could only wonder at that age why. How could daddy's stuff be here and he and mommy no longer talking? So why? Being so young, I got lost in cartoons and didn't put my mind to it until, well I gotta call. I'm wearing my favorite shirt, jumping on mommy's big bed. I picked up the phone and I'm asked if I know where my daddy is? Do I know how much daddy loves me? Not knowing I say "yes" to it all and quickly hang up. Everyone's walking around looking sad, but I'm still lost.

Time goes by, and I start to wonder. I can put things together and I know daddy's in a cell locked up between four walls. I know these walls won't let me see him. I know this is no happy place. My view of this world was different from that day on -- not because I felt alone or because I was the girl without her dad just like so many I knew, but because my rock had been taken. How would I grow up without the love of my father? How could I know who to trust to tell my days about? Who would be that person I feel safe with? I felt that maybe if people saw who I had become without him, they would give me back my rock...

Students sometimes wept while they read their essays. One young man wrote about losing his best friend. He had spent part of the day with her at the beach, and when he got home that evening, he watched the news and saw her body being taken off the beach on a stretcher. She'd been killed by a stray bullet. Half the class knew the girl, remembered the incident, and wept with him. The principal walked in on one particularly emotional essay and stayed for three more.

Students who completed that class began to proclaim to the rest of the school that it had changed their lives. If anything, their honesty with each other made them more open and hopeful, bonded them in their journey, and helped them stay the course when we began the harder work on Regents level analysis of literature, and afterwards when they struggled with their portfolios in their other classes. I wasn't the computer guy anymore. I had become their teacher.

In an alternative school where students have been kicked out or dropped out of multiple schools prior to yours, the balance between order and a living, learning environment is often precarious and dynamic. And it's individual: No two teachers manage a room the same way. You have to do what works for you while respecting the integrity of the overall community.

In our school, there was a "no hat" rule. I simply wasn't any good at enforcing it because I often didn't notice someone was wearing a hat until the class was nearly over. Also, I couldn't find it in my heart to pressure a girl to remove her hat when I knew that her hair was a mess and that was the reason she had worn the hat in the first place.

I remember a couple of times trying. Once, 45 minutes into a class, I said to a student, "Take your hat off."

"But I've had the hat on the whole time."

"Yeah, but I never noticed it."

Another time, I asked a student after the class had ended, "Did you have your hat on the whole time?"

"Yeah. You never noticed."

It got to a point where students simply laughed about my inability to realize someone was wearing a hat. It really was a waste of my energy to enforce, and two years later, the school dropped the rule.

Cell phones were another problem. Our City had a "no cell phones" rule. Yet, nearly every student had one. At the end of many of my classes, students took out their cell phones and snapped pictures of the board in order to record the notes. Also, students regularly googled topics we were discussing and sometimes even found more impressive supplementary material than I had come across. Occasionally, I ended up incorporating materials they found into lessons, sometimes impromptu -- lessons that I had spent hours developing -- which resulted in real teaching experiences for both the students and myself. Once, when I had a particularly small afternoon class, one student actually passed his cell phone around at my request, showing everyone a photo of what we'd been discussing.

I told students that I should learn at least as much from them as they learned from me, and if that weren't the case then something was wrong with the class. And I believe that to this day: any classroom where the teacher doesn't learn from his students isn't a healthy learning environment. Sometimes what I learned were little things about their world, which allowed me to tweak my lessons so that their world and my world would find each other.

One evening I found myself up at two in the morning reading and correcting papers on google docs, and I discovered that two of my students were online working on their papers -- only I soon discovered that they were together. We were able to "chat" across the net.

"Yeah. We together."

"Cool."

"What you doing up?"

"I'm marking your papers."

"At this hour?"
"Kids are asleep. Wife is asleep. Only time I have."
"We understand."
"I'll see you in class tomorrow?"
"Definitely."

The next day in class Mercedes wrote about being online at two in the morning with me while we worked on her essay. Guillermo wrote about it also. Other students in the class openly shared how I had chatted them up at different times as well. One student said that he saw me writing on his essay online but didn't know what was happening. He had just finished smoking a joint, and it had actually scared him.

"Man, it was like the computer was possessed or something."

After that, students wanted to find me online so that I could help them with their essays. And in class, there was a new sort of ease with me. They enjoyed what we did and were willing to take chances as they knew that we had created a safe space together. I told them that it didn't matter what their writing looked like at the beginning; all that mattered was that it improved over time. Put in the effort and maintain that effort; the rest would take care of itself.

I created lessons around relationships, using "Hills Like White Elephants" by Hemingway, where we examined why some relationships don't work out. In the story, the girl realizes that the man she'd been involved with doesn't want their unborn child, which represents her dream of their life together, so she bitterly decides to have an abortion. The word "abortion" is never used, and we talked about what often goes unsaid between two people and how the subtext of a relationship is often the driving force. That sparked all kinds of conversations about the difficulty of relationships, and their journals overflowed with rich portrayals of their home life, the struggles they had with alcoholic parents, with being gay and keeping it hidden, with boyfriends and girlfriends they couldn't possibly understand because of betrayals or reckless and destructive behaviors.

I structured a mini drug education lesson around a short story entitled "White Angel" by Michael Cunningham. In the story, the main character, only 10 at the time, gets high and drunk with his brother, whom he looks up to; in the end, he witnesses his brother, still high, run through a plate glass window and bleed out on the floor. As he was angry at his brother at the time and had a moment where he imagines he could have stopped him by uttering a warning, he ends up feeling guilty about his brother's death.

We used that story to examine how one single act could destroy an entire family, something that provoked stories of their own family tragedies, from drug overdoses, to shooting deaths of loved ones, to the murder of one parent by the other. One girl shared that she'd been living in a shelter with her entire family for the past six months; yet, she showed up for school nearly every day positive and ready to work. Another guy talked about how he'd backed away from a gang he'd been involved with just before his cousin and close friend ended up murdered. He felt guilty that he hadn't been there with them, imagining at times that he could have somehow prevented it; people pointed out to him, gently, how his actions had likely saved his own life.

Rules are tricky, especially when they don't reflect the reality of what's taking place. The balance becomes enforcing critical rules that support the educational community and your colleagues, while letting some of the smaller stuff go. How you, as a teacher, selectively enforce rules helps to establish your reputation.

The problem with relying on your reputation is that you have to develop one first. If you work in a big school that is well managed with general population students, while it can be difficult and it may take time, you have years of community reputation behind you as support. And you have well established school rules that you can fall back on -- rules that come with well-known consequences. In alternative settings like the ones in which I taught, you're sometimes thrown into the deep end of the pool, and it is up to you to sink or swim. Students can drive you out of teaching in your first year.

I was told that students don't care how much you know until they know who much you care. With the dropout population, they often have to learn who you are before they'll trust you. So despite my successes that first semester, I continued to struggle.

In my second semester back, some things actually got worse. I had this one class with seven Special Ed students mixed in with some of the worst behavior problems in the school. This class, which met at the end of my day, was the class from hell. I had the Special Ed students from the two major buckets: the learning disabled students and the ones with behavioral disorders. So one little thing, like sitting in someone else's seat, could cause a ED (Emotionally Disturbed) student to erupt into a murderous and cacophonous rage, activating other students who'd dance around the room in escalating forms of insanity.

I had two students, who probably had never had sex in their entire lives, continuously whispering about sex to each other. Day after day this went on. When one of my SPED kids sat in a behaviorally challenged girl's seat by accident (mind you, there were no assigned seats, only the seat someone claimed as his own), the violent eruption that followed set the entire class off.

After the dean removed the two students who looked as if they might kill each other, my sex-talkers went at it. I honestly don't know what set them off.

"Your dick is little!" one started yelling at the other.

"You're pussy stinks!" The other one yelled back.

Back and forth they went, yelling the same two things at each other with me standing between them, my arms holding them apart. When I turned for a moment to see what the rest of the class was doing, I noticed a third student filming the entire incident on his phone. I would be on YouTube the next day.

In this same class, I had one girl who couldn't stop talking, as if she had been stricken with perpetual diarrhea of her mouth. One particular day, she went off on such a nonsensical tangent to no one in particular that I actually envisioned myself calmly walking past her, slamming her head against the desk and then continuing to teach – as if nothing at all had happened. I had to physically step back from her desk and shake it off.

I had a young man who was transgender, and in our school he had begun to complete his transformation into a young woman. His attitude towards others was often caustic and rude – almost as if he had somehow internalized the contempt some others felt for him and then spit it back out into the faces of the rest of us.

His father once pleaded with me during Open School Night for help with his son.

"I just don't know what to do."

They had physically fought each other. I could only tell him that as a father, I had to constantly open myself to the possibility that my sons could be anything – especially my youngest who had a penchant for performance and had burst into song on a number of occasions.

I told this man, "Whatever else I might feel, I didn't want to not be there for my son – especially if his choices in life turn out to be ones which are beyond my understanding and perhaps even offensive to me personally."

When the talker, Alicia, and the transgender, Darnell, got chatting, my class literally ended. Each day, I felt my arm tighten straight into my chest while I tried to control myself and find solutions as to how to manage these ongoing situations and teach this class. I actually asked my doctor about the tightness in my arm.

"When does it happen?"

"When I'm in front of my class."

She laughed. "That's stress."

"You sure? I'm not going to have a heart attack or a stroke?"

"No."

I had my students write a paper and then create a presentation around their favorite interest. One of my worst students presented a piece about his pit bulls, where he spoke about what is was like caring for them, pausing to show the students photos of these beautiful animals. He could barely write, did almost no work in any of his classes, but when it came to his dogs, whom he loved, he got up in front of the room and presented. He also turned in a written piece that described his entire history with the animals, fully explaining why he loved them so much. After that class, he always felt that he could count on me, and despite what other teachers said about him, I knew that I could talk to him.

He took six years to graduate in a school that most students spend only two in, but in the end, he came to me for help to pass his reading and writing competency exams. Students need to be heard, to know that something about them is of value -- especially students who end up in a transfer school where they may already feel as if they are failures.

Despite all that I tried, the year remained difficult and discouraging. Monique frequently visited my room. She assured me that once I completed the year that I would be able to teach as myself again. If I gave up, then I was letting the kids beat me. Just hang in there any way you can is what she said to me.

Before that semester was over, my two worst students would give me my two best classes. Darnell, my transgender student, performed a scene from "To Have and Have Not" with a voluptuous

Dominican girl that the male students couldn't keep from touching. It's the "You do know how to whistle, Steve? You just put your two lips together and blow." scene. They were so convincing, and I had another colleague in the room at the time who confirmed what I had witnessed and felt. At one point, when they leaned in to kiss each other, it had gotten real enough that Darnell screamed as he was about to actually kiss the girl. The entire class loved it.

In another class, Alicia, the talker, opened up in calm and deliberate conversation on the topic of relationships, specifically abusive relationships. I always used the analogy that abusive relationships were like cooking a lobster. If you throw a lobster into a pot of boiling water, he'll jump right out – something I had witnessed as a child. My mother ended up beating the lobster to death with a broom, which is why I probably won't eat lobster till this day. But if you put a lobster into a cool pot of water, then gradually raise the temperature, the lobster dies without even realizing what's happened.

So when I followed that up by saying that abusive relationships where like slowly cooking a lobster, which is why people stay, adding, "If the first time you went out, the guy started pounding on you, you'd likely never go back, but if he gradually gets worse over time, when he crosses that line, you may find yourself stuck," Alicia spoke up.

"You think of all these things that you would do if your man ever hits you and then it happens. And I was just like, 'Did he just hit me?' And I didn't do anything. And then he hit me again. And I still didn't do anything. I mean, he hit me hard, and all I'm thinking is, 'This nigga just hit me and I didn't do anything.' I couldn't do anything. It felt like I couldn't leave him. I loved him too much. And I started thinking how I had done shit to him to cause this and that it really was my fault. I deserved it. That's what I thought. So I just stayed shut."

The entire room was silent. She looked up at me. "Oh, I made Joe cry." Is all she said. Indeed, tears were coming from my eyes. That class had the deepest, most meaningful conversation about relationships and abuse I ever heard amongst a group of young people.

By the end of that year, I could teach again. I began each semester's first class with this quote from Lao Tsu, "Failure is an opportunity." After a brief discussion, I further explained that people who learn how to handle failure are the ones who eventually succeed. I developed the reputation as one of the coolest teachers. Over the next two and a half years, students spread that reputation like a myth. They sold each other on my ability as a teacher. They made me into a near legendary figure who could inspire them to get through the English Regents. It didn't matter that it wasn't real. All that mattered is that they believed it.

The highest compliment a student ever paid me was to one of my colleagues. He said, "Joe is so cool I wouldn't even rob him." I did have the highest pass rate on the English regents semester after semester, and I helped more SPED kids to pass than any other teacher -- even when I had some sit against my colleagues' advice. One semester, a SPED student, Angel, who had originally come to us fresh out of rehab and barely literate, earned the highest grade in the school on the English regents. Of that, I'm most proud.

That is teaching -- only most new teachers leave the profession before they can experience the transition into managing a well run room where students help to create that positive environment where they can learn safely as at it can initially take a teacher two to five years to gain that kind of confidence; by then, as many as 50% have left the profession, perhaps even more in NYC. [1]

~

They come and go. Roads leading nowhere. People who at first are strangers, then colleagues, then even friends in moments are all of a sudden gone. They quit. They're fired. They retire. They grow ill. The move on. Some even die. And in the ever changing landscape of our educational culture, it is not just the students who are in constant flux, it is your colleagues, it is the rules, the standards, the requirements, the approach.

Everything is in motion, in perpetual change. One day you return and nothing is the same. You don't know most of your colleagues and your most endearing students have gone. You open your eyes and a young teacher is using language you don't recognize and it takes courage for you to ask: what is this new thing that you are doing? And when he explains it, you realize that it is what you've been doing all along, only you did not know its new name. For harsh and judgmental supervisors who question you, for state and city overseers -- often failed teachers and administrators -- you do not know what you are doing. And then you see that the new ones, the ones who can explain what teaching is, can't wait to leave the classroom, to become supervisors. Within five years they are moving on.

*You teach. You explore. You wonder. Each group is new. Each set of colleagues comes and goes. You remember the most painful of all, the startup school where two experienced teachers got pregnant that same year and left the classroom -- out of a staff of fewer than 10 -- just so they didn't have to say, "I can't do this. I can't work for this person under these conditions. Anything but this." One had begun the year endlessly going on about how she'd gone back to work so that her husband could pursue his dream. Now pregnant, **their dream** which she carried, allowed her to stay home and forced him to relinquish his dream without her having to openly say, "Fuck this. This is too hard. You get to chase your dream while I'm losing my fucking mind? Not happening."*

You remember that boss who made the frightening statement to the NY Times documentary team, "The problem is that I'm the only one who knows how to do this." In that moment you realized too late all was doomed. She'd never worked in a school before, never taught anywhere, and now she imagined as a one time educational director of a NY theater group she could conceive, execute and run a successful school. By herself.

You remember for a moment how things had gotten so bad at this job in just a few weeks that you once stood for a full minute at the top of a staircase, first considering and then trying to muster the force to simply throw yourself down in the hopes that you you'd be mildly crippled and wouldn't have to ever return to this place, to teaching.

After openly stating that it would take two years to know whether or not this startup school was working, she quit at the year and a half mark, citing the Department of Education as the reason for her failure. You were smarter. You drank and were gone within the first few months. This time saved by the bottle from the storm that raged inside of you. It would take two years to regain your footing, to get fully reinstated although you would be teaching again within six months.

You remember the road back, of sitting still with your five month old baby in your arms while this same former supervisor screamed at you for walking off the job. Screamed and stormed out of the room. For more than an hour. Back and forth. Screaming. Demanding to know why you didn't reveal you were in recovery, like her husband, a drunk. Screaming at how she could have helped you. Promising to sign your release and then slamming the pen down on the desk. Again and again. Her face up in yours across the desk. Then storming out once more, only to return.

You are asking her to formerly release you from a position you'd already lost, a position you could never regain. You are two months sober. Your sponsor in AA has already told you to let the job go; it's a consequence of your drinking. The Union has told you there's nothing they can do to help. Vocational retraining is what they offer you. Don't let the door hit you in the ass as you leave. You remember the pedophile they were adamant about defending. You must be worse than him some part of your brain exclaims.

She is screaming again as you cling onto your child. "What makes you think you can come in here and ask me to do this?"

And you say, "I heard that teaching is a very forgiving profession."

And she goes blank. It is something someone once said to you, and you do not know how it found its way across your lips. She is abusive, but you must swallow it, and the reminder why is held in your arms, and you cling to him dearly, tenderly, as a commitment to the level of humility you must now muster.

Not complaining that there were 45 students in your class when 35 was the max your contract allowed; not complaining but managing every single behavioral problem that arose as you knew were you to complain, as you had seen with your colleagues who did, you'd be viewed as "problematic", unable to manage your own class. Not complaining when HR from central office called and ordered you out of a building as you had never been officially hired -- you had worked there for months not knowing any of this -- only to have your boss, an assistant principal, tell you, "First, I need you to run a meeting with the staff. I don't care what central said."

You remember how your face burned as you looked around that table, wondering if they all knew that while today you were running this place, tomorrow you had no job. You lose your job that day.

Not complaining when you were asked to leave a building because troubleshooting a server was taking longer than you had anticipated, that your services were no longer required, but sneaking back in to finish the work without pay. Not complaining when you were offered four days of pay for five days of work for a full year to see whether or not you were worth hiring permanently. While at that same school another colleague, a personal friend of the Principal, was being paid full salary for her three and four days a week for that entire year as she had just had a baby. Not complaining. Doing your job. The job the new ones can't get away from quick enough with their supervisory credentials and the silent terror in their hearts at trying to manage 35 teenagers in the dropout environment in which you work: gangs members, drug dealers and thieves, abused and sometimes pregnant girls, viciously violent girls, and sexually abusive and sometimes violent boys, the terrified and bullied, the broken and lost: really, the deeply wounded, raging in pain.

You remember one of your colleagues, one of the younger ones saying to you, "You can't get involved in their personal problems. That's not our job." And then one day when she says openly in a meeting after you complained that too much was being asked of us, "If you're too old to do the job, then you should retire." She becomes a supervisor. You keep teaching.

Maybe you can't get involved in their problems on some level. On another level, their problems are the dynamic of your classroom. A human being who walks into a room imagining that high school math is the end all of what takes place in that room, without allowing the humanity of each to reach out and be seen and felt by all if only for a single moment of grace, whether its through a young woman standing at the blackboard with chalk in hand succeeding at something with the help of others or eventually on her own, something she had told herself, she had been told, could never happen, or if it's that wisp of light in the eyes of a heartbroken young man when you say to him, "It's okay today. Take some time for yourself. I'll see you later during lunch or early tomorrow morning and we'll catch up on this. Okay?"

The foundation of all education is that we learn to recognize and honor the humanity in each of us, in ourselves, and that we demonstrate this by the ways in which we treat one another. And if we can't live that within the constructs of an educational facility, within the decorated walls of a brightly lit classroom, then we need to tear down that institution and rebuild something else in its place.

---

[1] *Half Of Teachers Leave The Job After Five Years*, Huffington Post, 7-23-2014

Chapter Five

You Can't Teach

These are years filled with gray days. I feel precariously balanced between two worlds. In one world, I am married with a child and working as a teacher; in the other world, I am drawn toward my own destruction. When I drink, I find myself out for days at a time now, standing on corners on a Sunday morning trying to get a check cashed or in a dive bar hidden just off the highway where I drink and cop cocaine all night and day. I despise myself, and the longer I spend in this other world, the less likely it seems that I will ever emerge from it.

~

From year three to year fifteen, I worked in several sites of an extended educational community that frequently proffered advice to troubled students -- even though we, as a staff and as individuals, conspicuously had our own troubles.

Day one: I was a counselor. With college diploma in one hand and teaching credentials in the other, I found myself in an environment where everyone counselled students. None of us had any formal training as counselors – except the actual Guidance Counselors, one of whom was often mildly drunk, and the other, whose earlier education had prepared her to become a nun. Sometimes the forces that drove us allowed us to help; other times, these archetypal rhythms, these personal mythologies which defined who we are as human beings, got us into trouble.

Liam, who used alcohol liberally, truly cared for the students and felt righteously indignant at the tragically unfair lives many of our students led. I once rode with him from the day job to an evening job where along the way we stopped at his house, did shots of whiskey, and continued on with a guinness in each hand.

"These kids have almost no shot at life. Most of their parents are separated; it's not uncommon for a parent to be in jail or addicted to drugs." He sipped his Guinness.

"Some of these kids don't have a single responsible adult in their homes. The lucky ones may have a grandmother trying to raise them, but mostly these kids are pretty much out there on their own. Too many have been molested or raped by a relative. Or they're in physically abusive relationships right now."

Liam's words echoed a conversation I'd had with Rose, the other guidance counselor. "Our students are in survival mode, and left to their own devices, they're going to end up like their parents, repeating the same cycle: pregnant by 16, and then public assistance; they can spend their entire lives moving from one dysfunctional relationship to another."

They saw the exact same hopelessness.

Liam lit a cigarette before continuing. "Joe, how many students do you have who come in high every single day? How many of your students are pregnant or already have a kid? Look at the number of them who have serious weight issues or are grappling with depression."

He drew on the cigarette, held the smoke, then released it into the car. "We have students who struggle to make it to school because they're living in a house where people are up all night partying so they don't sleep. I got one girl sleeping on the couch in the living room while drug deals go on all night. I got another girl sleeping in her mother's room in the same bed with her mother and her baby so that they won't inhale the crack cocaine smoke that's coming from the living room. You really think they give a damn about school? Half of them are only in school because it keeps a government check coming into their house. They don't see it as a means to anything. And if you push them too hard too soon, they're out the door. They got shit lives, and they already know there's no way out for them."

"You really think they're trapped like that?"

"Maybe one in 20 will get into college and stay for a year or more; maybe one in fifty will graduate. Most don't even apply. They have to take jobs, legal or otherwise, to help pay the bills. I got kids in shelters with their babies, fleeing from abusive home situations."

I remember sitting in homeroom one day and watching one of my girls walk in late. I don't know what it was about her look, but I knew something horrific had just gone on. It's that other intelligence we all have that most of us so rarely listen to, which had kicked in.

I passed my homeroom attendance book on to a student -- something I had never done before or since -- and I called her over. These kids are smart in ways the rest of us could only dream about. The entire class kept chatting, like they always did in homeroom, and Juan took attendance while I spoke with this girl, but they watched me without my knowing that's what they were doing.

"You alright?" She shook her head. "You want to tell me what happened?" That's all it took. The girl couldn't breathe from the sobbing. When some of it passed, she spoke.

"The baby, my daughter, she wouldn't stop crying. She's only three months old. Pablo got real mad and started yelling at her, and I said, 'She's only a baby. She can't help it.' but that only made things worse." She was sobbing again. "He put his hand over her face until she turned blue." She cried that silent, shaking cry where no sound comes.

"Is your daughter okay?"

She shrugged. "For now."

I turned to Juan, "I got to take her somewhere."

"You do what you got to do. I got this." I looked around the room.

"Just go, Joe. It's under control," another student said.

I took her to Rosa, an office worker to whom I took all my troubled girls -- even though it's against DOE policy to leave a room of students unsupervised (not to mention having a student left in control of the attendance book, which is an official and legal document) -- and I had the girl tell Rosa the story. Rosa arranged for the girl and her daughter to be out of the house that same day.

I taught a parenting class once. One of the girls couldn't stand to be around her newborn. The mother had taken the child from her for fear that she would do the baby harm. In that class, she began to open up about having no feelings for her daughter, about not wanting to hold the child or to even see the child -- not even right after she'd given birth. I suspected that it was more than postpartum depression, that she'd been raped by someone close as she wouldn't talk about her mother's boyfriend who lived with them, but the why really didn't matter. At one point, she openly admitted to wanting the child dead.

Again, a trip to Rosa and to Rose, the guidance counselor, brought the young woman into counseling. I asked her to write about what she could in her journals, and when she first shared about having no feeling for her daughter in the room, the other girls, all of whom had children or were pregnant, recognized that there was something different about this. There was a tenderness shown toward her that she couldn't show toward herself.

Unfortunately, I would never finish teaching the parenting class or any class that semester. It marked my first trip to rehab. I started drinking one Wednesday and a week went by before I came out of it. I broke down and came clean in front of the Principal, and he pushed through an emergency medical sabbatical. I spent 17 days in a place called Smithers, (which is all my insurance would allow, and then only a few days at a time) a converted mansion where the daughter of the millionaire owner had hung herself after losing a prolonged battle with drugs and alcohol. Three months in aftercare and I returned that Fall fairly shaken and hardly whole. I knew that the guys who'd gone on to one and two year programs were doing what I needed to do, but my insurance wouldn't take me there.

The woman at the Board of Education who processed my reinstatement said two things to me: "Don't tell no one your business 'cause it ain't none of theirs; this is the only help they gonna give you, so if you go back to that lifestyle, you on your own." I remembered that when I relapsed a year later, not going for help because I believed that there was none. It nearly cost me my life.

Rose, who had once considered becoming a nun, wanted to save these poor and troubled youths that had been treated unfairly because of their race. She cared in ways few people really ever do. In an effort to even the score, Rose creatively awarded them credits for nearly everything.

"You see Joe," Rose once said to me as I was being trained for my new position as Coordinator of Independent Studies. "If a girl is raising her child, the hours she puts in amount to life experience. And I award her a credit just as if she'd taken a parenting class. You tell me what's more valuable: sitting in a class or the hands-on experience of caring for a baby?"

There were credits given for everything. A mother once said to her son at graduation, "They must have given you some of those credits for farting." Well intentioned as we were, we sometimes pushed the nearly illiterate and ill prepared out into the world with diploma in hand.

I once counseled a young woman on her relationship with her boyfriend. She was 19 and her mother hated the guy she was "in love" with. Barely a parent myself, I advised her to follow her heart and try to avoid getting into such open conflicts with her mother as she had to live under her roof. I didn't know at the time about how "live and die" teenage girls could be about everything. I hadn't learned that the surest way to drive a girl into the arms of a boy is to both despise him openly and forbid your daughter to ever be with him.

My own sister had married a guy perhaps in part because my father had forbid her to see him any more. He was Puerto Rican and we were Italian, an unacceptable match according to our Italian grandmother who ruled the family from the second floor apartment of our two family home back in mid 1960's Brooklyn.

First, my sister defied our father by going on vacation alone with him in Hawaii -- something thought of as indecent by our catholic family; then she held her wedding in the local church despite the protestations of both my parents. The marriage ended in a few short years after my sister proclaimed that her husband was boring and showed her no attention. By that point, my father had grown to like the guy and never forgave my sister for divorcing him. Go figure.

When I countered this girl's mother's warnings about the predatory nature of her boyfriend with, "You sound like you're really in love," and "I'm sorry that you have to struggle with not being together," I may have done the girl a disservice.

I would never see that young woman again. Several weeks passed before I asked someone what had happened to her. The answer shocked me: She had run away to Puerto Rico with her boyfriend, someone told me. One of the last people she had spoken to in the school had been me.

Another time, I ran into a student of mine on the bus; it was early morning and we were heading for school. I had wanted to speak with her about the young man she'd been sleeping with, a student whom I knew from two of my classes. In his journals, he revealed that he was sleeping with three girls in the school. The young lady on the bus believed that he was her true and only love.

The bus was crowded and across from us sat a wizened church woman. We spoke softly, but I knew church woman could hear.

"So how's things going with Rodney?"

"Oh, it's good, you know."

"You love him?" I never hedged on anything.

"I do."

"And he loves you?"

"He does."

"Listen, I don't mean to get personal, but I'm assuming that you guys are intimate. Are you're taking precautions." We taught sex education to our students and often spoke openly about these things, especially encouraging young woman to make sure that they used birth control, and with STD's running rampant, we pushed condom usage.

"Oh, he once pulled a condom out of his back pocket and he said to me, 'You see this condom. I use this with all the others, but with you, you're special.' And he put the condom back in his pocket."

"He actually said that."

"Yeah." She smiled. She was a 90 plus student, well mannered and beautiful.

"You do realize that he probably has said that to every girl he's ever been with, and there's a good chance that you were looking at the only condom he's ever owned."

"You think?"

"I would suggest you use protection."

The church lady started nodding. "You tell her. You put her straight." And she looked at the girl. "That's right, honey. He's playing you."

I saw her again when she was pregnant with Rodney's child and afterwards when she needed help trying to collect child support from him as he'd run off to the service and out of her reach.

In one school that I worked, we once spent days and days over the course of several weeks patiently explaining to an Armenian mother why it had to be okay that her daughter was gay, all the while listening to the poor woman explain to us how the father would literally kill this child were he to find out. I can't tell you how exhausted I came out of those meetings. Sometimes, the sweat would literally be coming down my face.

I worked closely with the Guidance Counselor, and I was released from class just to attend these lengthy and grueling counseling sessions. After six weeks of our best efforts, the mother pulled her daughter from our school. A year later, the girl returned to us about to get married. Turns out she had made a terrible mistake about being gay.

We did, however, accomplish one thing: we managed to get the NYCDOE to accept literacy in Armenian as meeting the state language requirement. That took two principals, myself, and several carefully placed calls to the Board.

We also discovered the same year that several of our female students were moonlighting as topless dancers. The guidance counselor and I joked about doing some "investigation" but kept seeing ourselves captured on the front page of the NY Post coming out of the place, girls in tow. The female Center Administrator weighed in:

"What are you going to do? They're all over 18. It's their life. It's their bodies. If they choose to make money that way, who are we to judge?"

Counseling overage high school students who had been kicked out of three other schools before reaching us was rather like giving advice to people who had already made up their mind about what they wanted to do; listening to whatever you said only strengthened their resolve -- whether your views supported their decision or not. Most often though, all these students really wanted was another human being to pay attention to them without judging.

Every one of our students had an emotional component tied to their inability to succeed educationally. If you couldn't help them crack that emotional nut, they weren't going to make it. That was probably the most profound thing I discovered as a teacher: if you couldn't help these students unravel key elements of their own self-sabotage, they weren't likely to succeed. It was as if they'd become tethered to an emotional knot deep inside of them, one that had eluded them up until now, out of which originated a variety of self defeating behaviors. These behaviors had, perhaps once been survival strategies but now no longer worked -- if this constellation of behaviors, and the nature of the core wound around which the knot had been tied, could even glimpse the light of their consciousness, then they had a fighting chance. Accomplishing this involved providing students with opportunities to change. Oftentimes, you ended up walking these students through controlled failures, but you never told them what to do. That truth they had to discover for themselves. Your job was to be there for them when it came time to pick up the pieces – if they indeed wanted to pick up those pieces.

We once had a student issued a summons by a police officer for using his train pass during the Easter break to get to our school to take enrichment courses. This young man had been in intense therapy at the time, and whatever his issues were, his psychiatrist now refused to be alone with him. He exhibited tendencies that worried all of us, so many staff members stepped up to the plate to support him through situations that lead him to anger. Our guidance counselor swore to us that he could be extremely dangerous.

When he returned from Easter break with this summons, still living in a halfway house, and fuming mad that he'd been singled out by this police officer when all he was trying to do was come to school, I assured him he had done the right thing by not hurting the cop, which is what he told me that he'd wanted to do. I further assured him that we'd get him out of this. I then took him to the Center Administrator, explained the situation, and she assured him that she would personally write a letter for him to take to court in order to answer the summons. Several other staff members spoke to him about the unfairness of the event, but assured him that the correct way to manage himself in the world was to let others help him.

When the judge dismissed the ticket, he turned himself over to us. When he graduated, we felt that he had at least half a chance. Left alone, he likely would have killed somebody one day in a rage. I felt as if we'd caught him at that critical point, had walked him through to the other side and had shown him another way that could work. The rest was up to him.

More than half the students who entered our school never graduated. They went on to other places: other schools, GED or specialized programs where they managed to circumvent the high school diploma; some left the state, even left the country; some went to prison; a few simply vanished.

Helping someone to successfully change proved extremely difficult -- no matter how obvious it became to the rest of us that an individual could not long survive remaining the person that he was. People are simply resistant to change irrespective of what life has thrown at them. I once offered a raggedy, putrid smelling, homeless man advice on how to get into a shelter as it was already late fall and life on the streets was about to become severe. This is what he said to me:

"I asked you for a dollar, not for advice."

Even while teaching in the prison, it had proven difficult to get through to anyone on any level. I never actually had a single student who had committed the crime he had been accused of. All my students were innocent. And they maintained their innocence at all times under every condition. Once, however, a student confided in me that while he hadn't actually committed the specific crime he'd been accused of, that in the past he had committed that type of crime on so many occasions that when he had finally been arrested, there seemed to be a certain poetic justice to the whole affair.

Students rarely ever asked you for genuine advice – at least with complete sincerity. There was always the thought that as an adult, especially a white adult, you couldn't possibly understand what they were going through. That level of trust rarely developed between you and your students without lines beginning to blur. Occasionally, a student might be so desperate that he had no one else to turn to, and then he might come to you and listen. Most of the time, a student just wanted to include you in his drama. It felt like case building with you as their supportive audience.

There's a certain magic to being a teenager. My recollection of it, often confirmed through observation, is that as a teenager, I'm unique: my world is the first of its kind. No one has experienced what I'm experiencing; no one can possibly understand what it is that I'm facing. In fact, I'm alone inside myself likely for the first time with a voice that only I can hear, and I identify that voice as me. Things happen fast in my world. A simple act can escalate out of control to the point that someone taking my seat becomes the jumping off point for what might result in a person going to the hospital.

I recall asking a student to sit down. That became a power struggle. For me as the teacher, I simply needed to establish order in the room. It wasn't personal. For my student, it became a matter of respect. There had been an edge in my voice that I hadn't been aware of; I'd fought with my wife that morning and still carried some of the frustration and disgust of that lousy encounter. The student had similarly come out of a struggle in his own home with his mom. My edge reawakened his battle for independence, and I found myself standing five feet from a teenager who had picked up a chair and was telling me that if I came any closer, he'd hit me with it.

The funny thing about it was that I never grasped the gravity of the situation. I simply looked at the young man and said, "If you're going to hit me with the chair then do it. Otherwise, sit down and let's get back to work." Thank God that when I edged closer, some other intelligence in me was able to read his body language and note that his flinching backwards with the chair meant that he would not simply hand me the chair and return to his desk. Instead, he tossed the chair sideways and stormed out of the room. Later that week, he wrote in his journal how he had been having a bad day and had argued with his mother that morning. He also noted that I had been having a bad day and had perhaps argued with my wife and that it probably wasn't a good thing that we both had had arguments and then ran into each other. He knew.

Months down the line, several students told me how I had the respect of the entire community. The assertion amazed me, and when I looked about as dumbfounded as a person can be, they referred back to the incident where I had stood up to Simon when he had threatened me with a chair. I felt speechless. I never really considered for even an instant that he would hit me with the chair – until I spoke to him about it. He said, "Oh yeah, had you come a foot closer, I would have clocked you with that chair." We were cool now and he felt safe saying those things to me. He would even one day come to me for advice about what to do after he had gotten his girl pregnant. He really didn't want any advice; he just wanted me to hear his thinking as he felt safe enough around me to share it aloud. Often, all a teenager needs is to be heard.

Even when my administrator had approached me about the chair incident, I simply told her, "He wasn't going to throw the chair. He was just letting off steam." When pressed, I said, "I never really felt threatened." I had just gone on and continued to teach the class after he'd stormed out. On my recommendation, no action, other than conferring with the student, had been taken. Sometimes ignorance of your reality is a blessing.

Besides, it hadn't been the first time I'd seen a chair thrown. A few years earlier while I was teaching on Rikers Island, a rather large student stood up after having been provoked for nearly two weeks by an equally large student, and he said this to me,

"Excuse me, Mr. Joe. But I'm gonna throw this chair at him."

This "chair" consisted of a chair/desk combo that weighed enough to make it improbable that it be hurled like a projectile. I had just enough time to step to the side when the chair/desk whizzed by my face and bounced off the wall. My two students fought all the way out of my classroom, down the long corridor past two other classrooms and into the vestibule outside the principal's office where they somehow trapped each other on top of a desk and into a corner. The next day we received a memo from the principal which read, "There will be no students allowed in the main office."

One of the next students who died really affected me. He hinted around in his journal that he often carried a gun out on the streets, which meant that he could be bringing one into the school, too. I spoke with him about it, and he tried to explain to me that it was dangerous on the streets of Bushwick, Brooklyn in a way that I didn't understand.

I had grown up on the streets of Brooklyn with some pretty rough characters. I had seen a lot of violence and a number of people had died around me. So I felt as if I could understand. What I didn't know at the time is that each generation faces its own struggles, and while there are undeniable similarities, there are differences beyond the understanding of another generation. I once heard it said by an older cat, "My generation wasn't afraid to die; this generation isn't afraid to kill." You can't understand that unless you're in it.

It's like looking at an abusive relationship from the outside and asking why the person stays. No explanation makes total sense to you because you are not emotionally rooted in that relationship; the other person is. A relationship is a living thing, an entity unto itself.

As a teenager, my world is both inside of me and extends somewhere outside of me. This is a new experience. When someone does something outside of me that affects what I'm feeling inside, I may experience that as having been violated. Depending on the nature of the violation and where I take it internally, I can even be willing to take a life or forfeit my own in order to save face.

You can't understand that unless you're feeling it. No words will make that meaningful to you; the volatility and rapidly changing emotional landscape that I live in as a teenager can sometimes feel like driving NASCAR speeds on a curvy mountain road. I can crash and burn because of what may look like an insignificant act, but at the speeds that I'm traveling over the terrain that I'm traversing, it's the nature of the beast.

In a relationship that has become abusive, I'm now mixed up with someone else in a way I can't separate or make sense of. And when my behavior escalates out of control or I accept the unacceptable, it's almost as if this thing that is happening between us *is us*. I can't control the other piece of me that has become this person, so I either strike out at them or accept what comes *as if the relationship is bigger than I am and now controls me.* In effect, I've lost part of myself. It now lives outside of me or at least it feels that way. And I believe myself to be completely helpless, whether I'm doing the abusing or taking the beating.

The teenage world is like this: I can feel helpless in the face of forces that compel me to actions I wouldn't ordinarily consider as this powerful and intoxicating, though unfamiliar, emotional terrain now both exists inside and outside of me.

One of the last conversations I had with the young man, Jarrel, went like this:

"Can't you step out of it?" I had asked him.

He said. "No." shaking his head while looking down. Then he'd made eye contact with me. "It's going down all around me. People want what I have and they're willing to take it from me."

"What if you simply quit carrying the piece?"

"I need it for protection."

"But it attracts the very thing you're trying to protect yourself from."

And then I told him my story.

"When I was growing up, no one carried a gun. Knives had come around and as we got older, a few of the kids started carrying them. That was dangerous. You just didn't get into a fight and shake hands when it was done, which is what I had seen growing up. You could get sliced in your face or even stabbed. Still, nobody was dying.

"By the time I had hit 18, it was pretty easy to get a gun. Things had changed that quickly. I joined the service and got out of town.

When I got back two years later, people had died, been murdered. A lot of others were in jail. I had carried a gun in the service, and I knew that I never wanted to pack one on the outside because it changed the way I did things. If I had a gun on me, sooner or later I would get into an argument and I would pull it out. I would put it to someone's face and say, 'Now what you gonna do?' And I had seen how those scenarios end."

"On my corner, two guys got into a fight, and the one that had been beat down came back with a gun. The other looked him dead in the eye and said, 'You ain't gonna shoot me.' And he turned and walked away. He didn't get five feet before six bullets were in his back."

I looked at him. "That's how it always ends."

He said, "That's real. So you know. It's just a matter of time."

A few weeks later, he'd been shot dead. One of my colleagues said at a service we had in the school that this young man could have been the next Malcolm X. I thought that that might have been a little over the top at the time, but as I got to know more about Malcolm X and recalled more of the conversations I had had with this young man, I realized that Mustafa, my colleague, had been right. We might have lost the man who could have been the Malcolm X of his generation.

As a teacher, you don't really know what you're teaching your students. This is not to say that you don't know what you're doing; it's just that you often end up surprised by what they walk away from a situation with.

It's difficult sometimes to separate literacy issues from intelligence, but they are truly rarely connected. So I may enter a classroom intending to teach literary analysis and end up with a group of students who learn how to manage conflict in a relationship. Many of them will learn to write in the process, but the thing they remember is often what you didn't even know that you were teaching.

In my early days, I was fortunate enough to work in an Alternative School. It had already changed greatly from what it had begun as. The old timers lamented the days, now long gone, when as teachers they had to walk the streets of Bushwick, gathering up potential students, convincing them to come into the building to try education one more time.

"Now we have 'intake.'" They said the word as if it were a form of cancer.

Still, teaching in an alternative school really opened my eyes. I saw the potential the right kind of educational environment had and all the possibilities it wielded. We worked in Bushwick, at that time, a nightmare of a neighborhood whose only saving grace was this Black Muslim community whose walkie-talkie carrying brothers patrolled the streets of their little enclave all day and night. No drugs were sold and no acts of violence could be committed within the reach of this community.

Our students themselves came from all over the city. I had a girl who traveled all the way down from the Bronx each day, and she was the first student in my class every morning. One day I asked a student whom I had failed why he was always late. He had wanted to know why I had failed him. I told him that he came so late every day that I often only had him during the last ten minutes of class.

"'Cause it takes me a while to get here."

"Where do you live?"

"On Knickerbocker."

"Where on Knickerbocker?" He gave me an address.

"Across the street?"

"Yeah."

"And you have trouble getting here on time?"

"It's not easy."

"To cross the street."

"No. I have trouble with it."

I looked at the girl who came from the Bronx and then said to him, "You know she comes down from the Bronx every morning. And she's never late." I turned to her. "How long does it take you?"

"Two hours."

"She travels two hours from the Bronx and is here early every day and you can't cross the street?"

"Yeah, well that's her. That's not me."

"How am I gonna pass you when you're not here and she is?"

"'Cause I do my work. "

"When you're not here?"

"When I am here, I do my work."

I looked at the Bronx girl again and told him, "If you can't make it here on time, I can't do anything for you."

"Well fuck you then." He said and got up and walked out.

The next morning, the Bronx girl sat alone with me in class as she often did, waiting for me to begin. She had never spoken before, but that morning she did.

"You know, if you had passed that guy, you would have never seen me again."

I stopped giving advice for years because of the girl who'd run off to Puerto Rico, but when I found myself looking at a teary eyed young lady from my advisory who sat in front of me, struggling with a father who wasn't in her life and a boyfriend who'd both cheated on her and then perhaps gotten violent, I shared a quote that had helped me in times of great difficulty: "Pain is the breaking of the shell which encloses your understanding." I further explained that her being in pain wasn't a bad thing; rather, she was waking up to a new understanding -- one that would help her to change if she'd embrace it. After the weekend, she returned with the full quote tattooed on her thigh. She even pulled her skirt up to show it to me. When I asked about it in front of one of my female colleagues, she explained that as it was such a long quote, she needed to put it on the largest part of her body. After a second young lady attempted to tattoo another quote from me on her back, I decided to revisit my thinking on the value of quotes.

~

I'd been sober for many years now, only I still raged inside, still hurt, still felt a deep shame about some critical core element of whom I believed myself to be. I overworked to escape my own sense of deficit; I did what others asked me to do out of a felt sense of obligation, out of the hidden, driving forces created during a less than ideal childhood, forces that had taught me, "In order to be safe, you must please others, you must be of service, of use, of value, to others -- even at the expense of your own well being. If you don't manage the emotional needs of others, they may harm you, even destroy you. You will be responsible for what goes wrong in their lives if you don't meet their needs." Of course, I didn't know this psychological architecture existed, only experienced it as a sense of being driven to overwork, to endlessly do and fix.

Abstinence from substances isn't recovery -- especially when it's replaced with other substances or behaviors which compel you. If I no longer drink but rage, overwork, over eat, over exercise, chain smoke cigarettes and drink coffee by the barrel, gamble compulsively, womanize or ceasely masturbate to porn to quell the emotional distress inside -- if I do anything compulsively, self destructively, regularly rather than face with compassion, with loving kindness, with equanimous presence, that which compels me to do, to act -- rather than simply be -- while I am clearly better off than I would be lying in the gutter with a bottle in my hand, I still live hidden from even myself in a life that is shallow and empty. I am in constant need of reassurance, regulation, nurturing, relief from emotional distress. And my relief in this paradigm only comes from outside of me -- whether it's from God or others or my great deeds or belief systems that promise me peace or salvation. In the end, I may in a moment of grace realize I never once took a chance on myself and tried living for myself, caring and nurturing myself first, getting to know, respect, support and love the being that I am that I might share that authentically with others.

That is the kind of education I needed growing up, that I would want for my children. If you believe in God, know that God is inside of you as this sense of presence exists inside of all of us. I am not God. That is different. My experience of God, my recognition of God as a force which shines through each of us, is what connects us all. There is no path to this.

My brother in law who spouted "Jesus this and Jesus that" for 20 years, with whom I had spoken in a deep and heartfelt way many times, respecting that his Jesus was his path yet seeing beyond that, seeing a similarity to what I had struggled to find, began meditating daily for a year and came back to me with this, "God is inside all of us. We don't need religion to tell us this."

And I said this back to him, "But Manny, and I never thought I'd be saying this to you, religion does help people, especially when they're really down and struggling."

He agreed but admitted that while he still attended church so as not to create an uproar amongst that community with whom he'd been close for 20 years, he now knew that God was everything and a piece of that presence shined through each of us, and we could connect to it by simply getting out of our own way. No one could take us there.

It is the same with education. Each of us has our own path. An ideal education ought to awaken us to the beauty and wonder of who and what we are that we might curiously, lovingly and most enthusiastically seek out means of self expression through a livelihood or a way of living. Most importantly, education as Gibran said, "... leads a student onto the threshold of their own wisdom." Who am I to imagine I know what that wisdom will look like for someone else?

Chapter Six

The Parallax View

W hy is it so hard to hold on? Why is each day its own struggle? There is a living darkness within. On good days, I feel life as a flow; on rough ones, I am Sisyphus, rolling that rock endlessly up the hill in my own private hell. Nothing matters. The hill remains unrecognizable except for that moment when I lose my footing and the rock escapes. As I watch it roll out of control, it is my life playing over and over again in its endless rhythms. In that wisp of a moment as the rock passes me, I know. I see it all. And then it is gone again. And I am somehow at the bottom of the hill, having learned nothing. Having to do it all over again -- only there is no ease in having struggled with it before. Each time presents its own challenges. In the end, I always fail. Even when I don't drink, when I don't disappear into that bottle -- and sometimes I manage for years dancing along the lip -- shame rages in me like a fire out of control.

    Each move I make or fail to make is dictated by an inescapable self loathing and the compulsion to escape it. There are days I close my eyes wishing that I would just be taken in the night, but with my eyes closed, a nightmare of a world comes to me. In the morning, I am exhausted but relieved that the ghosts and demons of that other world, of my inner psyche, don't call so loudly in the daylight. This *world, although at times painful and humiliating, unpredictable and confounding, has moments of joy and communion. The world of night, of three o'clock in the morning laying in bed with eyes wide open -- that world is far more frightening.*

~

    Teaching changes from day to day, from year to year, like shifting weather patterns, making it sometimes difficult, occasionally potentially deadly, and often unpredictable enough for human beings to easily acclimate. People in other professions see teachers as the beneficiaries of the 6 ½ hour day, the 10 month year, enjoying every holiday under the sun. Outsiders don't understand the powerful forces that bear down on teachers each day and the cumulative effects those forces have over time.

    One day you're just done. The day before you may have really had no clue that the next day you'd wake up unable to continue, having to cling onto your job, your sanity, your health, for the next few months, perhaps even years -- until you have to quit, retire or are dragged from the classroom in a strait jacket or handcuffs. Some of us end up carted out in a box or are dead within one year of retirement.

    First, the shortened day is a complete myth. New teachers can expect to take home a minimum of 10 hours of work a week for their first year. This is a conservative estimate. It can easily be upwards of 20 hours. Marking alone, if you're not careful, can easily eat up those first ten hours. Planning itself, which is far more important, requires even more time. It probably takes two hours of planning to execute one good hour of teaching – at least at the beginning. And the marking guides your planning; it is your window into who and what you're faced with.

    When a teacher executes a lesson, she is test running a new concept. There are a multitude of factors that make it new: it may be the first time she is teaching this particular lesson; she may have never taught it to this population before; she may not have taught it using the technological innovations of the day or she may simply have taught it during a longer or shorter time slot. Every factor impacts what she does and whether or not it will succeed. Even a specific mix within the same population requires a different sort of tweaking.

At the time of my retirement, "Universal Design" was the latest term that described creating multiple entry points into your lessons for a diversified student population. This alone could require hours of careful planning for one single lesson: gathering clever and interesting, perhaps interactive resources and then dividing the lesson into smaller learning sessions that use individual writing assignments, group work, presentation, and class discussion, etc... Then going home afterwards to reflect on how the lesson ran, what worked, why it worked, what didn't worked and why, to attempt to tweak the following day's lesson so that you can carry over somewhat seamlessly into the work you had intended or into the new direction, which has emerged.

And you may have taught the lesson to two different classes, where one went well and the other didn't. You ask yourself, what about the dynamic of this one class created the sticking points? Was there something different about the way you, as the teacher, presented the material -- even if it were subtle or completely unintentional? And why did things go better with the other group? And can you adjust the lesson to be taught differently to each class to keep them at relatively the same point in your curriculum? If one class simply has a better dynamic, can you enrich the next lesson, allowing yourself to keep pace with that other class, which you haven't figured out quite how to fully engage, so that the more rapidly moving class can open up into a deeper, more fulfilling learning experience -- at least until you unravel the teaching enigma of the less engaged group. Or do you even want to keep them in relatively the same place in the curriculum?

If you want to improve as a teacher, if you want to continuously provide meaningful learning opportunities for all of your students, this is what you do. And then some. There is no six and a half hour day. It's a fiction.

Like many caregiving professions, today's political and social climate requires that a teacher absorb a certain amount of abuse. A teacher has to take abuse. I knew of a professional screenwriter and accomplished author who entered teaching. In less than one year, he had been driven out of the profession. Jeffrey, white, worked in an all black school. The Principal had such political connections that his startup school up was named after his own Grandmother. One day in a fit of frustration, the screenwriter used harsh and admonishing language toward his students. His exact words were:

"Are you all a bunch of fucking babies?" He had dropped an "f" bomb on children who had cursed at him for months, dismissed him because he was white, talked about every aspect of his humanity, from questioning whether or not he was a "faggot" to why he wore such tight and ugly pants. It was a moment of frustration when he had grown tired of being unable to quiet a room full of students that he imagined he could actually teach. That first year can kill you.

The students bonded against him, turning to the Principal who then came after Jeffrey, and eventually Jeffrey was dismissed from the profession permanently for the use of "corporal punishment." That was the exact language used in the legions of papers compiled against him at his dismissal. He would never be allowed to teach in NYC again. Dropping an "F" bomb, while unacceptable, is not by any stretch of anyone's imagination, corporal punishment.

A lot of people think that when all else fails in their lives that they'll be able to make an easy living as a teacher. The old adage that "Those who can do; those who can't teach" drives them. Nothing could be further from the truth. There isn't anything easy about teaching. Most people across the country don't survive through their fifth year; in NYC, more than half are gone by the end of their fifth year and half of those after their first year.[1,2]

Gifted screenwriter or not, you don't enter a 9th grade inner city classroom and expect to impart knowledge. You need to learn from your students how their world works while attempting to seduce them into yours. And seduce is the proper term. Or con. Or trick. You have to do something to get their attention and respect or else you're dead. Just like with parenting, it's perfectly okay to cut deals: "If you guys give me these 15 minutes, then we can talk about doing something more relaxing during the next 10." Of course it's never 15 minutes. When students realize what's happened, ideally, the class will be well underway.

There is, however, a great irony surrounding the dismissal of a teacher from a classroom because he dropped an "f" bomb on a group of wild 9th graders who had been "f" bombing him for weeks – especially when you consider that in this country there are 19 states that on the books (Gershoff #) still allow a teacher to use actual corporal punishment on their students and significantly more that permit teachers to carry loaded firearms into their classrooms (Richmond). Harsh and admonishing language is not "corporal punishment." Being bounced off the wall multiple times by an adult, as I'd seen the Dean of my grammar school do many times when I was just a child, now that's corporal punishment.

My grammar school years happened at a time when there were no child abuse laws in this country – during the 1960s when men openly beat their wives, and children were brutally beaten by both parents, often in tandem. A beating at school from an official was kept quiet as you knew if you came home and told your parents, they would only beat you some more for getting that beating in the first place.

In the fifth grade, I attended religious instructions once a week at a Catholic school on Wednesday afternoons. Now, all of us were being taught by a Catholic school teacher, but we were public school children. I remember this kid, Fagan, giving the teacher a smart answer. She calmly made her way across the room and without any warning, drew her hand well over her head and sent it crashing down at the speed of light across Fagan's face. For the rest of that hour and a half of "religious instructions" I simply focused on the formation of red fingers on Fagan's face. Eventually, the complete and detailed outline of the woman's entire hand appeared like a work of art on his cheek. It remained there in perfect outline, until it dissolved into a red blotch. I heard not a word she said, and all I could think was that I did not want to provoke this woman in any way whatsoever. That was a skilled blow, one practiced and perfected over years of directed strikes.

We had heard stories of nuns putting chewing gum in girls' hair and the girls having to cut their hair off to remove the gum. We had heard of the prodigious paddlings from the Brothers who taught Catholic high school – demented pedophiles who had boys pull down their pants and bend over. My best friend had received this treatment again and again at the hands of a variety of sadists and pedophiles who thrived like vermin in the Catholic school system, overseen by the child molesting priests who wanted your "private and intimate" confessions to be ones you would carry with you the rest of your life. This single slap of a 5th grader brought back the reality of what danger we all were in back then at any time from any adult.

Our public school had a sadistic and maniacal dean who literally bounced students off stone walls until they were semiconscious. He did it again and again, often with the principal standing at his side, day in and day out, and we watched in both terror and horror as students were beaten senseless. But we knew in our hearts that the Catholic school system held much more ominous punishments.

Public school teachers might go as far as to put gum in a child's hair, and some of them got physical with you. Another friend of mine was once called to the front of the room where the teacher grabbed him by his hair and bounced his head off of the front chalkboard. All he remembers was the cloud of chalk dust that rose about him from the impact. That was how we grew up. There was no such thing as abuse; there was only what you had coming to you, and truthfully, most of the time you felt you had gotten off easily.

At home, my father stripped me naked and beat me down the stairs with a belt, threatening to throw me into the street "like the dog that you are" were his exact words. My mother beat me senseless. There were the simple slaps across my face or the more sophisticated onslaughts that generally involved a myriad of blows to my body – especially my ass – as she most commonly wielded a hairbrush that I eventually broke and surreptitiously mended in such a manner as to cause it to break from her next stiff blow. This way she might believe she'd struck me so hard as to actually break the brush over my back. I had become the dog who bites the slipper that has been used to punish him.

My first clear memories as a child were of falling out of the crib and hitting the floor. Now in this memory is the clear recollection that despite it was still daylight and I wasn't sleepy, I shouldn't have been escaping from that prison. Most imperative, beyond the aching bones from my smashed face and body against a hard tile floor, was the dire urgency that I somehow climb back into that crib and pretend to be asleep – all the while doing this both quickly and quietly before my mother entered the room and found out what I was up to. For in this memory lived the earlier memory of the vicious beating I had gotten for committing this same offense on a prior occasion. I had learned the lesson of punishment.

My Flight Chief in the Air Force once asked me at my first posting, "Airman, what does punishment teach a criminal?" We were police officers on an Air Force Base.

"To not do it again."

"No." this seasoned Vietnam Vet who had barely edged out of high school told my college educated self. "It teaches them not to get caught."

And the beatings I had already received by the age of two had taught me that precious lesson as well. I had to make it back into that crib and convincingly pretend to be asleep so that my mother, who would be standing over me in less than a moment, might not administer the beating I knew I had coming to me. I lay there quietly, feeling my bones ache, wanting to cry, but while she stood over me for an interminably long time, I didn't utter a sound. After she left the room, I sobbed for a long time into my mattress as my bones felt near broken, but I didn't get caught. I avoided that beating.

For us as a society to evolve into this culture that delineated between punishment, discipline, and abuse, moving the lines so far as to call dropping an "f" bomb corporal punishment and then using that single incident to end a man's career before it ever began spoke to the dangerous times in which we lived.

Children who shot and killed other children sometimes weren't responsible for their actions. It was their environment or society or mental illness or their underdeveloped brains that could be blamed. They weren't able to exercise consequential thinking, so how could we hold them accountable? They could get their hands on a gun, be pissed off enough to plot blowing away someone else, but you couldn't hold them accountable when they went through with it. Perhaps they were abused or neglected as children. Maybe they simply didn't have the opportunities afforded the rest of us. You still had to ask what kind of society had we become that we shouldn't even consider holding them accountable for their actions? The spouse or parent of the murdered victim often asked: what about my loved one? Where's my justice? Had the pendulum slipped too far to the left?

And when I say "accountable", I'm not talking about vicious and inhumane punishment. I courting the sense that we embrace a person capable of taking another's life before they'd even reached the threshold of adulthood and nurture them into a place, through directed treatment (treatment that probably doesn't yet exist), where they can grow into humane and loving adults.

A colleague of mine who had an unblemished record for the 26 years he'd been in a classroom, lost himself for a single moment one day. He'd been attempting to teach his math class in the midst of a pretty chaotic scene. The disruptions that consistently threw him off course came from one young lady who, after deliberate provocations from other students, would stand and state, "Well then, suck my dick."

Why a girl would say this proved baffling to the older generation who had grown up with that specific piece of foulness being male-owned for obvious anatomical reasons. Yet, of late, this abrupt assertion of one's distaste for someone had crossed genders, and now girls in our community let it slip from their tongues like sweet hellos.

It should be noted that the class had been getting what it wanted through these endless interruptions: to not be taught a math they had already failed at learning on multiple occasions. After a long series of "suck my dick" eruptions from this young woman, interruptions that held the teacher from progressing past the simplest mathematical concept, out of frustration he said the unthinkable.

"Well, I'll suck your dick if you'll just sit down and let me teach this class."

There is simply no way to defend this. Any explanations wouldn't make sense. How does a veteran teacher who's never crossed a line suddenly crash through the border of common decency, of moral and professional integrity, into that dismal zone of the unethical and professionally inexcusable?

Off to the rubber room with him. That's what we had in NYC – a "rubber room," a place where teachers who had gone off the deep end were banished and out of which they never returned: A black hole of bureaucratic debauchery where banished teachers remained on salary, sometimes for years, before going quietly into that goodnight. Over twenty million a year drained down that sewer while schools went on with oversized classes and a lack of resources.

NYCDOE teachers sometimes become warped by their years in the classroom, and in order to survive, to hold onto their income until they can make it to retirement, end up entrenched in some position that high explosives couldn't remove them from. Having an ineffective and high salaried teacher locked into a critical position where he is able to negatively affect the psyches of the young and vulnerable, the ones who need the most care, understanding, and help, is unconscionable, but these individuals refuse to quit even at the expense of their own well-being. And the UFT contract makes it almost impossible to rid a school of a tenured teacher.

To understand this inflexible and warped mindset, where one has been alternately battered on one side by whimsical and sometimes sadistic administrative tyrants and on the other side assaulted by the ever evolving dysfunctions of endless children, whose temporary insanity has often been empowered by an overly enlightened society, you have to look at the human relic that remains after 20 or 30 years; you have to witness the resolve of a prematurely aged psyche: this remnant of a person whose usefulness has long been outlived, who now simply waits to die or retire, depending on what comes first. To fully comprehend this, you'd have to hear one story from 9/11.

My wife's cousin worked on the 72nd floor of the tower that had been struck by the second plane. She had her back to the other tower when the first plane hit, but the blast from its impact lit up her entire floor so she could see the fire reflected off the opposite windows even before she turned to witness what had happened.

Naturally, they decided to evacuate their floor and her building. She headed straight out of the office, urging one older woman to join her. They worked for the IRS. This one elderly woman refused. She sat stubbornly at her computer terminal and said, "I'm not budging one inch from my workstation until I get the official word from downtown. These SOBs aren't going to dock me one dime for time away from work."

She died sitting at that workstation.

When you get old, you begin to feel that your usefulness has been outlived. And when you have spent decades of your life battling unreasonable and ever changing regulations that relegate your humanity to the nether regions of existence, leaving you clinging onto a position as you desperately try to hold out until you reach a level of retirement you hope inflationary unpredictability won't destroy – which could leave you eating cat food out of the can as I had seen older folks doing when I grew up -- then you have become a relic waiting to be discarded. All you have is what you can understand of "the game" that has been played, the one you can never win but now must somehow find a way to finish. You become the old woman sitting at the terminal, so bitter at the decades of petty micro managerial abuse, so afraid that your life, now nearly over, has really meant nothing. You become the staunch defender of what you imagine your integrity rests on, and you hold out against all reason. And you die. You die right at that moment.

What has always frightened me most about teaching is the sheer number of my colleagues I've seen die as they approached retirement or shortly after they've retired.

I remember Arthur who sang at our June graduation one year. He was a theater person who worked as a grade advisor. His performance at that graduation, which was also his swan song as he retired the next day, would be one of his last. He died within a year. And there was Joe Rodriguez, who sold real estate on the side and took lavish trips around the world during his summers. He lived well, had a beautiful apartment and vacation home, but one day I passed his office and noticed his head down on his desk.

It wasn't really his office. His office had been taken from him by a new administrator. Now he resided in some closet. (It literally had been used as a storage room up until the beginning of that school year.) After three or four days of noticing Joe with his head down on his desk, not moving, I said something to him.

"Joe. Joe." No answer. "Joe. Joe." No answer. "Joe. Are you alright?"

I waited. He didn't move, but this is what he said. "No." He was dead within a month. I guess he hadn't been all right.

The thing about a job is that you try not to identify yourself as being that job, the office as being your office and the classroom as being your classroom because in a real sense they aren't. In another way they absolutely define who you are, and when that stuff is taken away, many of us feel we're nothing. And some of us just die.

The city recognizes that it is unreasonable to expect the average human being to teach for 40 years under the current conditions and not transform into a caricature of his former self, perhaps discrediting his school and his city by acts of public insanity or ineptitude he couldn't be fully held accountable for, so they created an opt-out program called the 25-55, allowing still reasonably sane individuals to get out with a piece of an income. I opted out with 27 years a month before I turned 56 -- just in time to almost salvage my marriage and my relationship with my children.

When you think of teaching as the six and a half hour day, 10 month a year job, think again. I had a therapist tell my wife that most of her clients were teachers. Sure, it's not as dangerous by far as being a police officer or firefighter, but something happens to people who stay in the profession too long. They become caricatures of their former selves, and they often die prematurely.

Only my colleague, Ken, who managed to get out at 55 after 30 years, still seemed healthy. There was that one incident where he'd broken up a fight between two big girls who ended up taking him down to the floor.

After asking him if he was alright, I simply said, "You're about to retire. It'd be nice if you made it in one piece." Most of us don't make it in one piece. Parts of ourselves get lost along the way. Teaching is frustrating, sometimes heart breaking. It can break you. I watched one of my colleagues leave the classroom every single day crying. I taught the exact same class of students each morning, but by 12:00 pm, they were in rare form. Several of the students even said to me, "We made Lizzie cry."

"Why?"

"I don't know. Because we can."

"She's leaving the room like that every day."

"Yeah. She should probably just quit if she can't handle it."

"That's what you think?"

"Yeah. Why she gotta take things so personally? She needs to toughen up."

"You think it's okay to be so rough on her?"

Another student jumped in. "You don't take us personally."

"Yeah, well, I spent two years teaching on Rikers Island before I came here. There's hardly anything you guys could do that would bother me."

"Fuck you, Joe." I laughed. "See? Why she gotta get so upset at us? We just being ourselves."

"You do know that she cares about whether or not you guys do well. It's important to her that you succeed."

"So?"

"So show her some respect is all. She's trying to look out for you. You can't tell me you really feel good about her leaving the room every day in tears."

"Actually, it's kind of fun. That class is boring as shit."

Another group of students worked with the math teacher on remedial math. Since you couldn't give high school credits for a remediation course, they called it "Fundamentals of Math," but it really was just above adding and subtracting. When most of his class failed the Regents Competency Exam in June, I found him alone in his room, pacing and cursing.

"What's wrong?"

"They all failed. They learned nothing. Nothing."

"Take it easy. You did the best you could."

"They didn't learn shit. I failed them as a teacher."

As I left the room, he threw the exams to the floor and then jumped up and down on them. Early one morning, I would find him collapsed in the hallway sobbing about how he couldn't go on. I called someone who said he'd gotten like this before. I managed to get him out of the hallway into an office. A few years before retirement, I discovered that he'd been fired from his last teaching position, so I used some influence to get him one last position in my school. He lasted three more years, just long enough to accumulate enough time and reach an age where he could retire. Then the AP forced him out.

"Joe, we're not running a charity here." The principal said to me. "I understand you wanted to help the guy out, but we have to run a school."

I had always thought of him as a good teacher who had problems. I had co taught with him for a complete year more than a decade before and he had been solid in the classroom. In the end, they discarded him. What really went on in his room those last three years I couldn't say. I only know that there were at least three other teachers who should have gone before him. I had to ask myself if someone who'd been teaching for 25 plus years has anything coming to him in terms of consideration and understanding when he is no longer able to handle the pressures of a classroom. Or do you just push him out, and say that his retirement, his piece of a pension, is what he's earned?

If we throw people away, if we can't transition them into other positions when possible where they still have value, then we are dehumanizing each other on some level. We say, "This is a school and it has to run. And if you can't teach, you're gone." After 25 years? Isn't their mentoring he could do? Why do we hire the teachers who have escaped the classroom after as few as five years as mentors? Because it's cheaper than hiring a 25 year old veteran teacher? This was a good man living alone with his two adopted children whom he supported. He could have been an asset to new teachers, helping them transition into their first years in the classroom. That I'm certain of.

When I first entered teaching, people in the profession with 25 plus years were left alone. They taught to the rhythm of those years, seemingly asked by administration to do less than new teachers. It had been a right they'd earned through experience and seniority. By the time I'd accrued 25 plus years, the profession had changed so that I now found myself doing even more than I had done during my first 10 years as a teacher.

The idea of teaching for 40 years -- something that didn't seem uncommon when I'd first entered teaching -- under the current conditions is even scoffed at by the UFT. I once went on the UFT website and clicked on "career timeline." I had 25 years in. They had delineations for one year and then increments of five up through 20 years. For 25 years and beyond, the first subcolumn said, "Thinking about retirement." Even they know. Few individuals last 40 years in the classroom any longer without being some sort of anomaly or without sacrificing some integral part of themselves that leaves them feeling empty and lost when they're done.

~

Teaching is a love affair that tears at your soul, that burns a light upon both dreams and nightmares, that calls softly to you with sweetnesses that cannot be refused, but then bursts into cries of anguish as you watch countless others struggle to be born.

~

The dread that I will no longer be able to show up for my own life haunts me. I have been taught that the things I do, the responsibilities that I fulfill, are more important than I am. My only worth is derived from doing. Of myself, I am nothing.

I learned that lesson being beaten, naked, down the steps by my father at a tender age. The whistling of the belt against my body is a song I sang to myself, numb and on my way to school. Even after I am broken by the belt, by the threat of being thrown out into the world naked to die -- a world I no longer feel I can face -- I know I must go on.

I am tormented by the thought that other people will know what has been done to me, those faceless souls passing in the street beyond the solid oak door will have heard or the ones that saw me helpless and naked as I clung to the door knob in dawn's early light: They will know what I am, and still I will be forced to face them. It is too cruel and I shouldn't have to, but if I refuse, I will only be beaten more severely, in places which already ache.

I think my family might kill me one day, so I go to school. I get perfect grades, but the beatings come just the same. They are the song of who I am, of the incurable sickness that lives inside of me, that may always sing to me.

---

[1] *Why Do Teachers Quit?* The Atlantic, 5-10-2013

[2] *Half of Teachers Quit in 5 Years,* Washington Post, 5-30-2006

Chapter Seven

Peter Has No Principles

W*hen any of us believes that we can hold others hostage, that it's acceptable to make other people accountable for our lives, that's the beginning of crazy. Others may prompt us, may awaken in us, pain, but they do not cause us our misery. If they did, we'd always be helpless. In the final examination, it is our own pain, our own fear, our own needs, our own desires which drive us. Others may tap into that inner world, sometimes even with bad intent, but it is we who drive ourselves. Seeing this, clearly, non judgmentally, with compassion as this is the human condition is the opening into freedom and well being. We begin by freeing ourselves through forgiveness for having been so ignorantly and painfully blind. Life becomes at its best a journey into self acceptance, into nurturing and nourishing ourselves with tenderness, with compassion, with forgiveness -- especially when we have been unable to hear our own inner cries for kindness, for warmth, for rest, for love.*

~

What is education? Why do we educate our youth? In its purest sense, we want to raise individuals who are moral and self-assured, curious and open minded, loving and compassionate, independent beings able to create loving and fulfilling lives for themselves. We'd like them to earn a healthy wage in a dignified if not enriching profession or trade, an arena of self expression that also affords them enough freedom for enjoyment and adventure. We'd like them to know themselves in ways that allows for a natural respect of life.

Perhaps we'd like them to be literate in the ways of the society they are to one day help elevate and maybe even redesign. We might envision them as the architects of a better world where poverty, ignorance, disease, war, racism, and hatred -- the symptoms of despair and human discontent and the incontrovertible evidence that we have dehumanized ourselves and others -- are things future generations only study in history books. We certainly don't want our children repeating our mistakes. Education should be first and foremost about empowering our students.

As teachers, we are taught backward design. What this means is if I want my students to emerge from a class that I'm teaching with higher levels of literary analysis, with the ability to critically think and express this thinking through fluid and expressive writing, then I imagine what that will look like in a verifiable way. Perhaps it might look like this: I'd like my students to read two stories and then be able to craft an intelligently written and persuasive essay that uses their analysis of these stories to argue their point of view on a quote that I give them -- a quote they interpret in a way that their essay defends or refutes. Then I design backwards.

I work at figuring out every set of skills that will be needed to accomplish this measurable task. I keep working backwards, breaking down those skills into their subsets, until I get to an entry point for beginning students based on an assessment I must also design. Here's where we end up: After we assess Celia's ability to read, understand, and express her understanding through written argument, then we'll begin her journey toward literacy. That journey will begin with questions: Do we sometimes see the world differently than other people and if so, how does that affect us? Do we sometimes share similar points of view? What is a "point of view" and how do we use that point of view to direct our lives? What happens if we don't think the same way as someone else? How do we express or defend that point of view? What is an argument and how do we construct a convincing one? That might be an opening.

Our jobs as educators is to reach into our students' worlds and draw them out into the larger world, whether we do it using <u>Push</u> by Sapphire or Shakespeare -- even if we have to draw them into a world only they can imagine, one they may actually have to help create. To think of our students as anything other than the architects of the future that they will inherit is to fail to think of them at all.

Schools are sometimes imagined and then created using this same backward design: places where we want to nurture and challenge our students, to inspire wonder and creativity in them, to place the tools to create a better future in their hands and help them learn to use those tools with the hope that they may one day design better tools.

Unfortunately, the way education is currently designed, we often indoctrinate our students into our world, teaching them cynicism and racism, hopelessness and despair -- all the lessons of a society in open conflict. We impose on them a set of standards that we tell them are critical for them to attain with little regard for who they are as human beings or what they may actually want to learn; too often we do this with a total disregard for what they would be best served by learning. We tell them that this is the path; you have no choice. Instead of raising their hopes for a new future, we're either training replacements for this world or we're educating into these young minds an entire new set of problems: complex and insidious ways of seeing our society and each other that will haunt them for the rest of their lives, selling it to them as the solution for our current struggles. And we do this often with good intentions.

We lead by our bad example. They watch how we, as a society, can't get along. Whether it's teachers fighting one another or Unions fighting administration or all of us fighting state and federal regulations, they see many of the things which we say we'd like to get done, often don't get done. And that translates into a bad deal for them. Instead of our students being the most important people in the building, they often end up becoming an amorphous group we have to manage and maintain in order to preserve our existence as a school and our jobs as educators.

We punish them for failing to fit in, for failing to achieve, for failing to show up when not wanting to participate in the death of their own spirit might be the healthiest thing they could do. Society has it backwards.

Consider this: Our city and the UFT once stood at a four-year stalemate without a teacher's contract, letting hundreds of millions of state and federal monies go by the wayside while both sides refused to agree to an evaluation system for rating teachers required by the State and Federal Governments.[1]

An evaluation system for teachers seems like a reasonable thing, and how could any organization be effective that doesn't allow for the evaluation of its employees? The history behind the conflict isn't that simple.

Before this impasse, the City had begun gathering data for years on overall pass rates for students, by school, by department, by classes, and by teacher. They tracked students by economic class, by race, and by Special Ed status. The last thing they did was correlate all of the data so that questions such as these could be asked: If Johnny passed Mrs. Johnson's class, why didn't he pass Mr. Simpson's class? Mr. Simpson's pass rate is substantially lower than Mrs. Johnson's. Perhaps Mr. Simpson isn't as *effective a teacher* as Mrs. Johnson. Linking teacher evaluation to pay, which was one of the things on the table at the time, could result in Mrs. Johnson being paid more than Mr. Simpson. Once you create a financial incentive to pass students, it's freakonomics. Simply put, freakonomics argues that introducing a financial incentive into any system corrupts that system.

For teachers working in transfer schools, things looked more like this: How do I as a teacher hold my students to a standard most of them can't possibly attain in the time frame that I've been given with the constraints that have been placed on our school, the students, and myself?

In the Alternative school system, many students come to you after having been "passed" through elementary school without adequate numeracy and literacy skills. According to my retired colleague, a former speech therapist who taught JHS, fixing this required required more resources than were available, and she often had to fight the administration for the monies necessary or use her own funds and personal time to get the job done. Her explanation of what went on in junior high schools -- how students sometimes entered sixth grade having not achieved basic literacy and fundamental numeracy skills, with the JHS most often being unable to "catch them up" -- helped me understand why students who entered our high school seemed years behind. By the time an educationally crippled student reached a transfer high school, he's additionally struggled for two or more years in at least one other high school.

Most of our students were age 17 and had few credits. How can we catch them up? How can we as a school raise the literacy levels of these students to where it should have been had they and their prior schools been held accountable for the first nine to eleven years of their education?

If we, as teachers, as a school, ignored these realities and held students to the standards we were being required to impose on them with the current resources available to us in the time frame allotted, then the majority of them would continue to fail. As teachers, we'd be rated ineffective, and as a school, we'd be deemed "failing" and eventually slated for closure. Putting aside my personal stakes, how can I reasonably hold a student accountable in three years for the 10 years of education he never received? That's the conundrum.

The City and State wanted an evaluation system for teachers that links teacher performance with student success: graduation rates, pass rates in classes, and competency levels on state exams. Such an evaluation system would allow the Department of Education to eventually dismiss teachers who aren't effective and close schools that aren't succeeding as measured by these metrics. The Union appeared to want as little accountability as possible so that it would be nearly impossible to fire anyone.

Both the City and State independently of one another already possessed the power to shut down "failing" schools based on attendance, pass rates in classes, competency on state exams, and graduation rates. When the powers that be created a teacher evaluation system, which directly links student performance to teacher effectiveness and considered adding financial incentives for those who succeed while stiffening the consequences for those who fall short, they forced a conspiracy between school administrators, teachers, and students in order to ensure everyone's survival.

So teachers pass students because they're pressured to by administrators, by other teachers, by their own consciences or by the need to survive. And we convince ourselves we're doing a good thing or at least the lesser of two evils. Sometimes, state exams are generously marked, especially with graduating seniors, and credits are magically found or granted for those same students. Other times, cheating takes place -- whether it's the erasure of answers, the doctoring of transcripts or the changing of grades.

The point here is that instead of educating our students in a meaningful way, we're often stuck trying to push them through a system that simply doesn't work for them.

While the City, State and Union couldn't agree on an evaluation system for teachers, letting huge sums of money go untouched, consider that NYC schools like ours had just experienced three straight years of budget cuts.[2] Cuts of any kind almost always cost us people on the ground. As a school, we couldn't hire as many teachers or we lost office personnel. Fewer teachers meant larger classes; fewer office personnel meant more paperwork for teachers and less time devoted to students.

While schools struggled financially, it seemed ironic that the ways in which the DOE did business wasted schools' money. Budget cuts resulted in less equipment and fewer supplies; yet, the method by which the equipment and supplies were purchased still hadn't been called into question.

At the time, the Department of Education's purchasing system was designed to only allow schools access to vendors they approved of. You could only buy items from vendors on the DOE's list of approved vendors and then only the DOE approved supplies and equipment, which these vendors listed. If you needed a piece of equipment that the DOE didn't approve of, that became a juggling act of monies and paperwork. If you wanted to purchase an item the DOE did approve of but that you could find cheaper someplace else -- or perhaps a better version of it through another vendor, which was often the case -- that required getting three bids from three separate vendors and then submitting paperwork requesting permission to go ahead and use school's monies to make that purchase. Sometimes, your payroll secretary neither had the time nor the inclination to walk you through the process.

At one point, in order to purchase Apple computers, you had to buy them through Dell, their competitors, as Dell had landed the contract with the city to sell technology to all NYC schools. This would result in the purchase of Apple equipment that was often two years older than what was currently available on the market. To make matters worse, it wasn't uncommon for six months to pass between the time a major technological purchase was made and when it got delivered into your hands. The equipment your school received, while brand new, was nearly technologically outdated.

Another huge waste occurred whenever you made major technological purchases. You had to pay an installation fee for having individuals simply take the equipment out of the box and connect the equipment to your network -- something your tech person had to do almost every day -- and if your school received a grant from the city, you had to hire a consultant before you bought anything, a person who was supposed to advise you on what to purchase. If you had your own resources, persons on staff capable of taking a computer out of a box or a technologically savvy individual capable of figuring out what was needed to install 50 computers into a building, you couldn't use these individuals – at least you couldn't get away with not hiring the consultant, which cost you a percentage of your grant, and the guys and gals who took equipment out of the box at $35 a pop. Eventually, the DOE conceded to you the competency of removing laptops from boxes on your own. The consultants, who often did next to nothing, remained, their fees built into the actual grant as a "kick back" cost.

On the pedagogical side during this time period, pairs of teachers who were tenured but had lost their positions at other schools for a variety of reasons would be placed in schools throughout the city for two weeks at a time, continuously being replaced by two others throughout the entire school year. These individuals were on full salary but did nothing meaningful. Some were used to cover classes; others were asked to collate documents or make copies. Mostly, they just sat around.

If a school wanted to use them, said school would have to take over their salaries; otherwise these pedagogues who had come from recently closed down schools or had been excessed – or even let go for poor ratings – would be ushered on to the next school and so forth, until they saw 20 plus schools during a single year. The city paid their salaries, the union guaranteed their employment because they had become "tenured," and we couldn't use them because they were gone by the time we trained them, so as potential resources, which we desperately needed, they went to waste.

The shifting of these "excessed" teachers from school to school was reportedly designed to allow schools to look at these individuals and potentially hire them; however, it often played out more like the city's super scheme to dishearten these individuals, perhaps even to shame them into resigning or retiring. Many teachers took their free money and kept on going.

We once had two elderly and nearly insane ATR's (absent teacher reserve, as they were called) arguing by the copy machine about their prospective incomes and personal situations. It looked as if it was an argument that could have taken place in an asylum. They stood face to face yelling at each other as if no one else existed, while teachers and students passed them.

"I told you personal information about my finances. How could you use that against me!"

"Leave me alone! I told you to leave me alone!"

Both appeared to be desperately crying out for help, but no one paid any attention to them. They could have been a married couple fighting the battle that had locked them together for decades. We had a school to run, were in between classes, and there simply wasn't enough time. I probably should have stopped to say something, but I couldn't risk being drawn into their madness. Instead, I remember resenting them because they were earning the same salary as I was, only I didn't even have time to eat lunch while they could stand around all day creating problems for the rest of us. And that's what many ATRs ended up doing: they became nuisances to the schools that they'd been placed in, endlessly pestering office staff, teachers -- anyone who would listen -- in ways that made it apparent to the rest of us why they'd been dismissed from their former positions in the first place.

Tenured teachers facing charges were a whole 'nother can of worms. NYC had a rubber room where teachers accused of misconduct awaited hearings while still on full salaries. At one point, it was estimated that over $20 million dollars each year went to pay the salaries of teachers in the rubber rooms, some of whom remained there for upwards of three years. Some estimates raised the monies being wasted between the ATR's and rubber room to over 100 million per year.

School lunch was still another fiasco. Across the city, tons of food got thrown away each day, but as with major restaurant chains, you can't give away your waste; you have to bag it and put it out on the street. We probably could have fed the entire homeless population of NYC each day with what we tossed in the garbage from all NYC schools combined.

In my early 20's, I read a book entitled <u>Tools for Conviviality</u> by Ivan Illich. In it, he discussed how the structures of a society and the mechanisms within a society impacted on individuality and psychological well-being. In one section, Illich uses the example of a worker on an assembly line, stating that this worker has had his humanity subordinated as he is taught through the repetitiveness of his job that this mundane task is more important than he is. This Illich felt was a direct consequence of industrialization. Illich went on to discuss the consequences of institutionalizing learning and healing and how that created a monopoly on education and medicine in a way which disenfranchised family and culture. Your aunt's home remedies are no longer good enough; your father doesn't know what he's talking about as you are being taught something different in school.

Illich pointed out that the layout of a building itself affected the people inside of it, noting that the architects who designed prisons also designed schools and hospitals, and that struck me to the core. How many students have said to me that being in school *felt* like being in prison? He went on to say that when a government monopolizes education, it creates consumers of education. The ones who succeed receive more education; the others are punished as a consequence of their failure.

I've always argued to many of my students that with economics and race working against so many of them, education promised to be the great equalizer, the one thing that could open any door for them. Yet, I worked in schools that were most often under equipped, understaffed, and lacked quality resources -- resources readily available to schools in well-to-do neighborhoods. My students, inner city children mostly of color and from poor economic backgrounds, weren't blind either. They spoke about how LaGuardia High School had an ID system where you swiped your card and attendance was taken while my students had at one point homemade IDs -- ones that a colleague and I had run off the computer and laminated ourselves. In the end, it may be the things we often never consider that have the longest lasting impact on our students. When students who barely have enough to eat watch as food is tossed in the garbage each day, it leaves its mark. When those same students see excessed teachers in the halls being paid $100,000 a year for doing nothing while their own families struggle at poor paying jobs of endless hours just to make ends meet, it sends a message. When they're given outdated equipment fresh out of the box, we are telling them something about their own worth. However, the greatest waste committed by any educational institution is that system's failure to properly address the needs of its students, to nurture the untold potential of those individuals -- whether it be by poor design or lack of resources. When City, State, and Federal authorities battle with local unions and each other, allowing hundreds of millions of desperately needed dollars to go by the wayside, it is the students who ultimately get the short end of that stick.

We shape the future society through the ways in which we educate or fail to educate our youth. When we teach our children racism through the inequity of their public education, we teach them about their own insignificance; when the adults in charge of the wellbeing of children and young adults fight each other rather than find ways to serve their charges, the lesson is clear to our students: you don't matter.

Most crimes I believe are committed by individuals who have learned to dehumanize comfortably. Is it a coincidence that these same "criminals" have been educated in a building designed by architects who also design prisons, force fed an assembly line styled education more reflective of a society that existed a 100 years ago, punished by a curriculum that fails to address the needs of the most vulnerable amongst us, and taught by professionals who are themselves dehumanized by this system which both employs and constrains them?

~

I have learned through meditation, through yoga, through t'ai chi, through qigong, through compassionate and reflective journaling, through gratitude lists and daily wisdom readings, through actively pursuing the longings of my heart and supporting those pursuits with daily practices of health and well being, that it is I who need to change, not the world. When I change, the world changes. It really is both that simple but that difficult.

---

[1] *$100 Million Wasted Per Year, and De Blasio Doesn't Care*, New York Post, 8-10-2016

[2] *Ivan Illich - Tools for Convivialitys*, MOM Ediçoes, 5-31-2011

Chapter Eight

Losing Everything

It is early Sunday evening, the sun settling low in the sky, and we are still in the Brooklyn Botanical Gardens. I am hungry, and despite all the beauty around me, all I can think of is how we are on the wrong end of the gardens. The walk home will be long, then I will need a bath, and bedtime will come shortly after supper with no time to play. Already, that Sunday evening dread, which I will carry with me my entire life, has taken over, and every part of my being wants to slow down time.

It's only today I realize that there were no beatings on Saturdays and Sundays, only during the week. Why, I can't say. And the dread I will feel all of my life, that I have felt each day I rose for school or for work -- it is learned.

~

When I was 10 years old, my fourth grade teacher took an interest in me. Back then, your entire school day consisted of sitting in a single room filled with desk-seat combinations bolted down to the floor in strict rows. With the exception of lunch and recess, we never left our seats.

My father was still beating me back then, stripping me naked and whipping me down the stairs -- always threatening to throw me into the street, "like the dog that you are." The beatings had become sporadic by then, with long enough respites between them that they sometimes faded from memory. I remember this one particular morning, after an unexpected and severe beating, sitting quietly in class, sure that some of the bruises were showing. My teacher, Mrs. Rothenberg, paused by my desk. I stiffened at her scrutiny, praying that she wouldn't ask me about the belt buckle mark on my face where I still felt the injury quietly pulsing, and she didn't. Instead, she later called me over privately and asked if I'd be willing to come in mornings early to clean the boards and wash the erasers. I agreed.

The beatings at home stopped after that. I can't tell you why. Once, Mrs. Rothenberg asked me what my parents thought about my report card. I had all E's for excellent, except for handwriting, which should have been an "F" but understanding my plight, Mrs. Rothenberg had given me an "S" for satisfactory.

"My mother wanted to know why I'd gotten an "S" in handwriting."

Mrs. Rothenberg face jerked backwards. On my next report card, although my handwriting hadn't improved at all, I received an "E" in that also. She again asked what my mother thought of the report card, and I replied that she had said it was better. Mrs. Rothenberg shook her head as she walked away.

When Mrs. Rothenberg asked me what my mother thought of my performance in the school play where I'd landed the lead role, I repeated what my mother had said. "How come you didn't play the other fellow?"

"What other fellow?" I had asked my mother.

"You know. The funny one."

"But I had the lead part."

"Yes. But it wasn't funny. You're so funny."

I hadn't known with all the beatings that I received regularly at home from both my mother and father that either of them ever found me funny. What I remember most about my performance was having to sing, "When Irish Eyes Are Smiling" beginning off stage and continuing until I came on stage, and my singing got plenty of laughs. That and the fact that I'd forgotten one line during the performance in front of the PTA and had stood there looking blankly across at my fairy costar, who'd whispered in anguish, "You idiot. My mother's out there."

Her admonishment had both shamed and infuriated me, causing me to immediately jump to the next line I remembered, something I would later discover was the preferred method of professional actors who found themselves in the same predicament. When I think back on it now, I can see that much of my life I felt as if I were standing in front of a harsh and critical audience where I'd either forgotten my lines or had delivered the wrong ones.

I tested gifted that year. Had been offered a special school to excel at my own pace. It was the first time some of the kids and I spoke as four others had tested gifted as well: "You going."

"No."

"Me neither."

"I don't want to be in a school taken away from my friends and with a bunch of nerds." That was from my fairy costar. In that silent room where the only voices you heard were in answer to questions, you never really got to know anyone.

In fifth grade, Mrs. Rothenberg made me part of the school's honor guard, where I carried the flag out in all assemblies. She wrote a graduation speech, which I delivered. I went on to test gifted for a second time in Junior High School, to skip the 8th grade and move on to Brooklyn Technical High School where I became a chemistry major. Two chemistry teachers later after my adolescent attitudes had repeatedly clashed with their aging sensibilities, I found that I'd lost all interest in becoming a scientist, and wound up lost -- only to wake up one day as an English major in college. In graduate school, I'd find my calling as a teacher -- though I have sometimes wondered what my life would have looked like had I pursued science, which I still love.

What I remember most about P.S. 124 is how Mrs. Rothenberg somehow touched me in a way that preserved the remaining bits of my integrity as to affect how my own family treated me. At least for a little while. She taught me the power believing in a person can have. I would employ that model as a teacher, and when I found that my ability to think of my students in that way had begun to wane because perhaps I had become overly concerned with my own survival, I retired.

Fourth grade had been the year of the teacher's strike of 1968 when schools had closed for the first 36 days of that school year. The strike would end in a disaster, with teachers losing two days pay for each day that they'd been out; additionally, teachers would be forced to make up the lost time. Our school day would now extend past 4:30 pm, previously ending promptly at 3:00. There were moments when Mrs. Rothenberg's frustration slipped through.

"That stupid Union." She once said as she left the building at nearly 4:40 in the afternoon, racing to catch the Long Island Railroad to return home. "If I'd had any idea what they'd do to us, I'd never went along with it."

And there were other times when she lost it inside of the classroom, screaming at one poor child who showed up on assembly day with a wrinkled white shirt.

"What did you do? Sleep in your shirt! My lord, it looks as if you did sleep in that shirt."

The boy sat there through it all, appearing half asleep. Mrs. Rothenberg's compassion got the best of her again, speaking to the boy more quietly. She had another student escort him to the restroom where he washed his face while she ironed his shirt herself in front of the classroom.

One day a young lady, Eva, came in wearing fishnet stockings. The first time I'd ever seen Eva, I'd felt embarrassed for her. It must have been the second grade. She was Latin, and and had what could only be described as a mottled complexion. I'd seen black people and latin people before, but never anyone with a creamy cocoa complexion, as if smears of color covered her face. I thought she'd simply had forgotten to wash her face. How else could you explain that complexion? I remember how concerned I'd felt for her, for the embarrassment she must be feeling. I myself had allowed my face to get much dirtier than hers, but I would never come to school looking like that.

In fourth grade, when she came in wearing fishnet stockings, Mrs. Rothenberg blew a gasket. She went as far as to exclaim aloud to the class, "Why, you're dressed like a whore!" I thought I would die from the embarrassment I felt for her. I also couldn't keep my eyes off her legs. It was the first time I'd ever noticed a girl's legs.

The halls often echoed with the screams of teachers admonishing their students. Faces got slapped, students humiliated and beaten, and sometimes teachers simply lost their minds. Mrs. Riley, an obese and perpetually red raced Irish woman whose stockings strangled her puffy thighs as her skirt rode up around her hips underneath the desk but in plain view of the middle three rows of her class (as was far too much else), would fart repeatedly every time she lost her temper. It played like a symphony of yelling and farting, her face increasing in redness, making it appear plausible that she might actually explode. That was 1968.

~

Today, teaching remains an endless exercise in patience and self-control that pushes ordinary people past limits they never realized they possessed. In one moment, a word or deed can cause you to cross that line of propriety and perhaps lose everything.

This was the case with Sean, a math and art teacher who had an unblemished record for his 26 years in the classroom. One day he ended his career by repeating out loud what a student had blurted out in his classroom 10 times in a single hour, standing each time to disrupt his class. Off to the rubber room with Sean.

Sean's story became the cautionary tale, the story teachers in my school told to each other as a warning of what could easily happen to any of us. What stands out the most for me was how disoriented Sean became by the swiftness at which his life had changed. I ended up taking over his Advisory after the permanent substitute was let go, so I got to examine the full scope of his last 20 years of teaching, which had taken place in my last school.

He had extensive records kept for two decades of teaching. Every student who'd ever passed through his classroom, through his advisory, through his life, had left some record, some mark imprinted upon Sean. There were endless photos of students who must now be in their 30s and 40s, standing with a young and exuberant Sean. His love for what he did shone in his eyes.

There were the boxes and boxes of files, of portfolio assessments, of endless student work that I would have to, over the next three years, deposit in the trash. I felt as if someone had died and I was clearing away the remnants of their life.

And there was the art. It was beautiful. Some of it belonged to Sean himself, who clearly was a talented artist, but much of it belonged to past students. Eventually much of that would go, too. His books on art remained and his one costume that he wore each Halloween – that remained too. He had dressed each year as the killer in "I Know What You Did Last Summer." No one knows any longer what Sean does with his summers.

Math books, hundreds of them, all teaching math in some way that it was no longer fashionable to teach -- all that had to go too. I'd toss out two or three books a day, some of them brand new, others hardly used. At one point I had gotten rid of more than 100 large bags of garbage, uncovering a beautifully stocked art closet that held treasures teachers would die for: paper mache, oil and water based paint, paper, markers, charcoal, scissors, crayons, colored pencils, printing materials, mesh, matte, stenciling equipment and a complete setup for creating custom t-shirts. And that was just a small part of what I had found.

I had an art teacher come in part time, a professional artist, and together we used the contents of his closet to create projects that enhanced my students' literacy and eased the ache in my soul over the death of my colleague's career.

Even more striking than the thoroughness and organization of those years as evidenced through his record keeping were the conversations I'd had with him before he disappeared past the event horizon of his teaching misconduct.

"I just wanted to teach my class." He said to me one day outside of the building. He'd come, after all the students had left, to clear out his belongings.

"What happened?"

He told me the entire story. "This girl kept jumping up in the middle of my lesson, yelling 'Suck my dick." I was just trying to teach the class. Other students would get her all worked up, and she'd jump up again. I couldn't teach anything. So finally I said, "I'll suck your dick if you just let me teach this class."

It was unthinkable. He couldn't even believe that it had come out. "It wasn't even the girl who reported me. She told me that she didn't have any problem with what I said. I mean, I know I shouldn't have said it."

"Who reported you then?"

"A girl who was failing my class. Someone who never did any work at all. One of my own advisees. She'd been bitter because I'd already failed her for cycle one and now she was failing cycle two."

"I don't understand."

"The rest of the students either denied that I had ever said it or said to the Principal that it had been no big deal. My own advisee had made the stink about it. She went home and told her mother who then called the school."

"You're telling me that this girl went out of her way to get back at you?"

"Yes. I apologized to the girl who I had said it to. She had no problem with it, and she admitted that she had been way out of line by constantly jumping up in the middle of the class. I mean, I was just repeating back to her what she had said to the class and to me."

"Yeah, but you crossed a line."

He had trouble with this. While he knew he had, he almost couldn't believe that it had happened. In that moment when he'd uttered those words, he didn't recognize himself. "I just wanted to teach my class." Is all he could say.

He had had enough. He looked and seemed old and broken, well beyond his years. It was sad, painful, and frightening. You were left asking yourself would you make it to retirement? Or would you, one day in a fit of anger or frustration or just plain insanity, lose it in front of your students and then ultimately forfeit your livelihood forever? It seemed too cruel.

How many lines had I crossed but escaped consequences? Would I cross a line one day in front of a single student who hated me and then have that student capitalize on my indiscretion in a way which resulted in the end of my career? After decades of an onslaught of intermittent abuse and love, would I simply crack and then have the remaining pieces be swept off into some corner of obscurity?

There had been so many others before him during my tenure. I remembered my partner in the computer lab, Rodney, a 26 year old colleague whose young wife wanted a divorce because she'd found success in music and her own beauty salon. His wife had grown tired of living in the shadow of Rodney's mother, a retired school administrator who had raised several children and a husband.

Rodney, in the midst of this separation, found himself vulnerable to the ministrations of some 19 and 20 year old female students who needed his "counseling." As one of my administrators once told me, "Your counseling methods were more designed at meeting your own needs than those of your students." That woke me up.

Rodney found himself "caring" for some of the girls in ways that crossed lines. It's inexcusable, yet it goes on, and we know we shouldn't be doing it but there is some unmet need in us that has found an unmet need in someone else, and we are drawn to that person, that place, against all reason.

I once read that the love between a teacher and a student is quite real and should be honored; it's just that it never should be consummated as this is a violation of the ethics of your profession, and it is up to you, as the professional, to make sure that those lines are never crossed.

Eventually, Rodney moved in with an ex-student, a 22 year old graduate from our program who still had friends in our school. That is where the real problems began. The young lady, now proud she was living with her former teacher, made sure she kept up her relationships with her girlfriends who still attended the school. So they called each other frequently, the students actually ringing her up at Rodney's home. The girls got playful and began to harass both Rodney and his live-in with calls in the middle of the night. Rodney went to the Dean and asked for his help.

"Look, I'm living with a former student and her girlfriends keep calling my house at two and three in the morning and harassing us. I think they're high when they call. These are current students of ours. Can you please put a stop to this?"

The students were simply being playful with the calls, but when the situation came to the attention of the Principal, and in the light of a recent public incident where a 26 year old teacher had taken a 16 year old female student on a road trip across the country "for her own protection," things got serious very quickly. Rodney was relieved of all classroom duties and a full investigation was launched.

I was to be the star witness as Rodney and I had shared a computer lab together. The first time the investigators called me in, they asked me technical questions about the operation of the lab. In those days, it had been possible to send messages across the network, from a machine in front of the room where Rodney often stationed himself, to any student operated computer in the entire lab – or to all the computers at the same time. Allegedly, Rodney had been sending secretive texts to one or two specific students, little private sex-texts that only the girls and he could see. They wanted to see the record of all these texts. After I checked the system thoroughly, I explained to them quite honestly that the system simply didn't work that way: the program saved no record of any communications between machines.

Next, I was questioned about Rodney's behavior. Had I ever seen him do anything inappropriate in the school with any of the students? The answer was "No." I hadn't. Quite honestly, he never seemed to notice the young ladies, some of whom I thought were stunningly beautiful. I said as much to a student one day when we were leaving the building together and her response was this:

"He didn't have to look at them in school if he could have them after school."

Had I ever seen him with a group of specific students in the school? That was the next line of questioning. In the lab, yes, I told them.

"How often was he in the lab?"

"Almost all the time."

"Was that normal?"

"He worked in the lab and operated it better than anyone else in the school except maybe for me. He used it effectively and he assisted me while I taught my class sometimes. I appreciated the help."

"Was he supposed to be in the lab?"

"He didn't have to be. He either was preparing his own work or helping me with mine as I often helped him out when I wasn't troubleshooting something else in the building."

"What about these girls? Did he seem to pay unusual attention to them?"

I remembered one specific girl who seemed to hang around him. Once I had left the building through the back door and found her leaning into the window of his jeep, talking with him about something. But they weren't asking about her. They were asking about three others, the ones who had been calling his house, harassing him and his live-in girlfriend. So the answer was no.

They knew that he lived with a former student, who was now 22 years old, but apparently they couldn't do anything about that. She had been out of the school for more than a year before that took place.

The case continued to develop over time. We worked in a program that had six sites in four boroughs. While we graduated more students than some of the bigger, more prestigious high schools in the city, we weren't a diploma-granting institution. State funding was being cut for all programs like ours, and the principal of our program had opted out of the opportunity to turn us into an actual high school.

Up until this point, we had collaborated with City as School, and once all the academic requirements for graduation had been met, City as School granted our students their diplomas. Because of the cut in state funding and our failure to become a school, we had been slated for shutdown that June.

Rodney's case continued, however, and from time to time, I got little pieces of information about what was happening to him either when investigators managed to track me down at the new school where I now worked or whenever I made contact with my former administrator. It seems that just before we were shut down, the three girls in question -- the city's main witnesses against Rodney – had been pulled from our school permanently by their grandmother and aunt who both said, "I'm not going to let you girls ruin that man's career over some silliness that the three of you pulled." The elderly and wizened women went on to say, "You had no business calling that man's house, harassing him." These women, seasoned by much living, told the investigators that their nieces and grandchildren would not be allowed to say another word against Rodney.

One fall afternoon while I sat in a computer lab in Brooklyn in between classes, a call came through. It was the lead investigator on the case. We talked for quite some time, and then I asked him point blank, "What evidence do you actually have against Rodney?"

"We have a strong case against him."

"Yes, but if you don't mind my asking, what evidence do you have to make that strong case?"

"We have the girls' testimony about things he said to them."

"On the phone."

"Yes. On the phone."

"When they were calling his house in the middle of the night harassing him."

"Yes."

"I heard that the grandmother is refusing to allow those girls to say anything."

A silence followed. "That's true. The grandmother and aunt have been very vocal about not involving the girls."

"So the girls aren't going to be witnesses."

"Not unless I can sway the grandmother."

"I don't see that happening, do you?"

He hesitated. "No. Not the way things are right now."

"So what evidence do you have?"

"We have you." He said.

"Me?"

"Yes. You're our star witness."

"But I've never once seen the man do anything inappropriate with any of those girls."

"We have a case."

"If I'm all you've got, it seems to me that you don't have anything on him at all."

A long silence ensued. "Be ready to testify. You'll be called upon to tell what you know."

"But I don't know anything."

"We'll be contacting you."

I attempted to contact Rodney against the instructions of the investigator to let him know that they didn't have a case against him, but he never picked up the phone, never returned my calls. I heard later that he, too, had intended to call me as a witness on his behalf, but it never happened. Instead, he had been pressured to resign in lieu of charges being pressed against him with the stipulation that he never again be allowed to teach in NYC.

~

I still remember Mr. Grande, the Spaghetti Bender, as he fondly called himself because of his Italian heritage. It was seventh grade and I was in an accelerated program with other gifted students. One day he simply lost it with us. We'd always come in after lunch, half of us eating, most of us talking, and on this particular day, he lit into us. Perhaps things had happened earlier that day; perhaps he'd simply had enough of trying to settle down what was supposed to be the smartest class in the school each day after lunch for more than 10 minutes before he could actually teach anything.

I can't remember what he said, but he yelled at all of us, said things that hurt deeply and caused us to feel ashamed of ourselves for not having lived up to our potential. He spoke for five straight minutes, a pained look on his face. I'd felt afraid to even move, never having seen this kind and gentle man in this state before. At the end of the speech, just before he exited the room, he said these simple words that resonate in me to this day:

"Joe, erase the board." Somehow, he hadn't been talking to me. I had been spared. When he returned five minutes later, he simply began to teach. Teaching was like that. At any moment, the best of us could lose our minds. And it seemed that there was absolutely nothing that could be done about it.

Chapter Nine

Teaching Wasn't Always This Way

A*ll my life, when things have gotten tough, I've run. In a group therapy session, I was once asked to recall an example of courage, but could not; at times, my life has felt like an endless series of defeats where I fled from one humiliation to another, sometimes narrowly avoiding complete annihilation. Maybe courage for me has been the resilience to reengage despite these shame filled and self-destructive episodes.*

~

  I attended a public school that had one male teacher who was also the Dean. My kindergarten teacher eventually became the Principal as I would discover on my visit there 15 years after I had graduated and just before I would enter teaching as a profession. The Dean, now much older but still menacing, wouldn't be bouncing students off the walls. Most classrooms were no longer set up in rows; instead, desks in groups of four served as "workstations". Students had portfolios instead of folders.
  On my return visit, I felt that while things had changed, they hadn't truly innovated as I had seen in Central Park East, a small

public school in Harlem that I had also visited at the time on the recommendation of my advisor from the graduate program at City College where I would earn my Masters degree. Although CPE was suspiciously populated with a disproportionate number of "white" students in what was still an almost exclusively African American and Latino neighborhood, the school looked unlike any I'd ever seen. I visited a third grade classroom and watched one teacher alone manage 25 students who appeared to be engaged in a variety of activities. One child sat piling blocks in the middle of the floor, building an enormous structure, while another sat reading silently to herself. Others worked in small groups or moved freely from activity to activity.

"You're just going to let him sit there all day doing that?" I asked about the kid piling blocks. We're talking about a pile three feet wide and nearly as high. I figured the kid must be special.

"Until he gets tired. Then he'll move on to something else."

The teacher explained that students in this setting had been allowed to progress at their own pace in a variety of subjects. This young man, for instance, who sat quietly piling blocks by himself, I had been assured would one day soon excel at mathematics. The "constructing" he engaged in evidenced his proclivity for math.

"How is reading taught?"

"We do some phonics, but essentially we allow students to learn from context. It's a more holistic approach." Skeptical that an eight year old understood the word "mincing" as in "mincing along behind them was the princess." I asked the girl who sat reading to herself what the word meant.

She looked up at me as if somehow curious about why anyone would ask her that sort of question, as if no one had ever asked her the meaning of a specific word before. She repeated the word and my question before answering.

"It means that she's walking with little steps like a princess."

Later in the class, the teacher transitioned everyone into a group activity. Students were making masks of themselves. This required that one student lie back in a chair while a second student administered wet strips of paper mache to the first student's face. The entire class worked in pairs or as individuals once they no longer needed each other's help. I felt speechless at the order and ease with which these students worked with one another, neat and gentle. It was a thing of beauty to watch. I had great hopes for where education might one day go.

There were still no computers visible in any classrooms in either of the schools. The internet was in its infancy and technology as a tool consisted of television, movie projectors, a VCR, and the overhead.

One thing that struck me about CPE was the concept of what an elementary school should be: It was a place of self-discovery where you not only learned fundamentals, but more importantly, you learned about yourself through creative exploration and expression.

CPE had begun with just a few grades, adding an additional grade each successive year. That year had seen the first sixth grade class, populated by some students who had been with the school since its inception. They intended to add a seventh and then eighth grade, their argument being that the transition into JHS for just three short years before high school was simply too disruptive. There had even been discussion back then about creating a Central Park East High School by adding a grade at a time, using the original CPE as a feeder school -- ideally following the same model of self-discovery through exploration.

When I first entered my elementary school, there had been a 6th grade, and students moved from this relatively peaceful setting into a JHS, which had a 7th, 8th and 9th grade. My brother, 10 years older than me, told me that he had completed 9th grade in JHS, and his high school, which had consisted of 9th, 10th, 11th, and 12th grades, really had only begun for him in the 10th grade. It had been the same for my older sister as well. Parochial schools had a different idea. You went straight from kindergarten through the eighth grade in the same school, which was the model CPE had discussed adopting. From there, you moved directly into a Catholic high school that had relatively the same values and culture as your elementary school, at least in theory. You knew what to expect.

Public middle school -- grades six, seven, and eight, became known to me as the place you ought never teach. It seemed that chaos and insanity sometimes ruled -- even in the two middle schools that I attended as a pre-teen. There were fights outside of both schools on a regular basis. And after I'd become a teacher, I once witnessed a full blown riot outside the middle school downstairs from where I taught. During the riot, only one single teacher from the middle school emerged to help. Perhaps the rest hoped the students would simply kill each other off.

It had been rumored that the one-armed Vietnam veteran who taught there once hung a kid out of a window, threatening to drop him if he didn't start behaving. Not only were the students nuts, it appeared that the teachers themselves could easily lose their minds.

There's a strong argument for not allowing junior high schools to exist independent of other schools. Students in that age group are simply hormonally imbalanced to such a degree that they are capable of anything. Bunch them up in a new and somewhat out of control environment and you have the average NYC Intermediate School: it can be chaotic and violent, much of which largely remains under reported on a public level.

I worked in a high school above a JHS. Two incidents come to mind. Once, a pretty, well-mannered young lady -- a student in our high school -- was beaten by one of the JHS students until her face was an unrecognizable pulp. The girl who had perpetrated the beating wore her victory like a badge of honor. My student, after having climbed the stairs back into the building with a welted and knotted face that continued to swell as we spoke, never returned to us out of fear and shame. The child who had administered the beating had been egged on by her bloodthirsty peers, teens driven by forces few of us have ever known but for perhaps shadowy moments in our lives.

The second incident remains perhaps one of the most horrific scenes of violence I have ever witnessed in my life. Two of us were looking out the window at the end of our school day when a group of students stormed from the building. They happened to form a circle two floors beneath us and a simple fight broke out. When you work in a school, you know that these things are going to happen. Some staff member always knows, but no staff from the school downstairs emerged. Instead, the crowd grew larger.

For a while it looked simply like a girl fight, but once one of the girls got knocked to the floor, people in the crowd began kicking her and then stepping on her. The other girl who had gotten up, began doing her best to stomp on this girl's face. It all happened so quickly that my colleague and I had remained spellbound. We were joined by the guidance counselor, who, once he had seen what was going on, decided to go down and rescue the girl before she was killed.

At one point, my colleague, a Vietnam Veteran, the custodian, another Vietnam Veteran and I looked at each other. "Liam's out there alone."

"We got to go get him."

So we went after the guidance counselor. By the time we had reached the street, a full fledged riot had broken out. These two Vietnam veterans were pushed against either of my shoulders, and the three of us entered into that frenzied mob as one force. Hundreds of students were screaming, littering the streets in a frenzy, throwing anything they could lift. The girl had made it to the corner Bodega with the help of the one friend she seemed to have. Charlie, the Dominican store owner, wouldn't allow the part of the mob that wanted to kill the girl into his store. He stood strong. At some point, we found Liam, the guidance counselor.

He stood angrily in the midst of this chaos, and at first, resisted our best efforts to move him. It was as if in defiance of the insane violence around us, he refused to budge. He simply stood, angry and transfixed in that one spot where the girl had lain. When we managed to move him, we saw that a teacher from the JHS had attempted to rescue the girl from the Bodega and then, under fire of rocks and garbage, placed her in the back seat of her car with another girl who had been helping her. The beaten girl appeared to be in and out of consciousness, having to be carried most of the way across the street.

As the teacher attempted to pull her car from its parking spot amidst the hundreds of maniacal beings who populated the sidewalks and streets, a cinder block carried by two of them was hurled through the back window of this teacher's car, completely shattering the window and landing on the two girls in the back seat. The teacher, beeping her horn and driving slowly but steadily through the crowd of possessed entities who had once been children -- demons who blocked the street and banged on her car -- managed an exit. Both girls were admitted to the hospital. Shortly after her departure, the street thinned out and rather quickly no one could be found. Then the police arrived.

We were later told that the police had waited in their patrol cars two blocks over until the carnage was done. I shudder even writing this down.

This insanity that occurs when you uproot someone from their elementary school and thrust them into a JHS environment, often carries on into the lower grades of high school. Students who are just

13, 14 and even 15, tend to be less predictable and more volatile. Take that population and put them into a prison setting, and it's cruelty beyond your imagination. On Rikers, even the adults often cornered an adolescent about to age-out of that population and enter into the adult population with this warning: "Don't try none of that crazy shit with us 'cause we ain't having it."

Working with 13 year olds in a prison setting was about the worst population you could imagine. My second summer with incarcerated 13 to 16 year olds proved particularly dangerous, nearly deadly for me. It was the only time I have ever been openly attacked by a student.

I had studied kung-fu as a young man and managed to practice some of its basics for some time into my 30s. My new class at summer school, which consisted of mostly Latin and African American students, contained two Chinese kids who had jumped from a boat, which had grounded itself off Queens, NY as they had attempted to enter into this country illegally. Only a week before summer school had begun, the Chinese students had started a riot in the pool hall that had been used for recreational purposes. They actually broke pool sticks over people's heads and hit others in the face with pool balls thrown as hard as one could hurl an object. People had their teeth knocked out.

These were dangerous people who had no fear of anything that could be done to them. They'd just spent months hiding in the hull of a ship in order to be smuggled in from China, so they could care less about the guards in this place. This prison was a paradise by comparison.

One of the Chinese students would threaten me on a regular basis. It became so intimidating for me that I began to go home and practice specific kung-fu moves that I had been taught years before – just in case. I remember feeling the stress at having to face another day locked up with this student. It wasn't what it had been the summer before when a principal whom I knew ran things in far more orderly fashion.

It's difficult to explain what it feels like to be locked up. Even though you get to go home at the end of the day, you're still locked up for the entire day. If the prison officials do a head count and the numbers don't come out right, the prison gets shut down. Everyone remains locked in until the numbers come out right.

On several occasions, teachers were kept in the prison for more than 12 hours straight while DOC endlessly counted the inmates. A wrong head count was most often simply that: someone hadn't counted correctly. The real concern was that someone had escaped.

The first summer I worked at this facility, I had felt safe. My principal had a good relationship with the Department of Corrections person who co-ran the school with him. Students were well behaved or else immediately disciplined and even removed from school if they had been deemed a danger. The second summer wasn't like that at all, and I found myself working in an unsafe environment where anything seemed possible. So I went home each day practicing a specific series of kung fu strikes designed to counter the aggression that I anticipated would eventually come from this student.

One day the young man simply picked up two pencils and walked up to the front of the room and raised them as if he were about to stab me through my chest. The kung fu kicked in, and I reflexively chopped him across the neck, causing his head to bounce off the blackboard. I was probably as shocked as he was, and in that moment of pause, he grabbed me. A few moments later, we were wrestling on the floor and I had him in a headlock where I choked him out. Two correction officers rushed into the room and waited for me to release him. When he tried to stand, it was clear that he had been nearly unconscious.

This kid vowed to get me back. After that, I had to watch him even more closely. Under different circumstances, he would have been suspended and removed from my class, but this was not the case here.

One day when I was working at my desk during a prep period, I heard some banging on the door. You learn in a prison to ignore a lot of different things. And this was one of them. Anyone who wanted entrance into the room had a key. Anyone else simply didn't belong. The banging continued, so loud and persistent that I actually got up, but when I glanced through the tiny window of the door and saw it was the student I had choked out, I brushed him off and went back to working. He became violent, kicking the door furiously and screaming at me. I simply blocked him out.

That day, he and several other students escaped from the prison. He had been on his way out of the building and had stopped to pay me one last visit, presumably to exact his revenge. Had I opened that door,

I might not be here to write this. Out of all the students who escaped that day, the two Chinese students were never found.

~

  I entered kindergarten in September of 1963. My sister, Veronica, deemed uneducable only three years before, had been refused an education at this same school. A principal could make that call. Veronica would later be diagnosed as emotionally disturbed and mentally retarded, a term we no longer use today as it is considered perjorative. Back then people simply said, "She's retarded." Sometimes she was referred to as "the retard" by the less delicate amongst us, such as the guy who ran the Sweet Shop across the street from my house.
  "Your sister's the retard, isn't she?"
  "Don't call her that. That's not nice." his wife had said.
  "Well, that's what she is, isn't she?" He turned to me. I sat at the counter sipping on my three cent seltzer water fresh from the tap. "The boy knows it."
  I nodded my head but felt a burning inside. Somehow Veronica being retarded had been a blight on our entire family, almost as if it might be contagious or perhaps symptomatic of something more insidious going on with all of us. As a family, we kept to ourselves. When I entered elementary school, I felt eyes on me. They didn't want another retard on their hands.
  The educational structure of my elementary school would be considered coarse by today's standards. Classes were organized by student intelligence, from 4-1 to 4-3, with the one classes being considered the smartest and the three classes being thought of as stupid. Some teachers in my JHS, where this structure had continued, actually referred to the 7-3 students as "stupid". I remember my seventh grade science teacher explaining what it was like trying to teach these students:
  "These are the dummies, like a step above retarded, though I suspect some of them may actually be retarded. You learn more in a day in this class than they learn in a month." We were all laughing. "They might get a job as a garbage man or digging ditches or carrying heavy objects for someone else -- something that doesn't require any intelligence."

In my elementary school, teachers could and often did hit you. Mostly it was the Dean who "disciplined" you. I once saw him choke out a student in a headlock. The kid was in one of the three classes.

In the 1960's, special education seemed to be a largely private affair. The only specialized public education that existed was the 600 school, a lockdown facility populated by mostly black and Puerto Rican children. [1] My parents, Italian and Russian by ethnicity, weren't going to send their disabled daughter to a school designed to house criminally minded minorities. The thought frightened them almost as much as having a mentally disabled child had shamed them.

From what we heard as kids, the 600 schools were where they sent you if you couldn't be managed. It seemed like some cross between a reform school and a prison, though the Board of Education itself used this language, "THE "600" SCHOOLS ARE DESIGNED TO EDUCATE EMOTIONALLY DISTURBED AND SOCIALLY MALADJUSTED CHILDREN WHO ARE RECOMMENDED FOR SPECIAL PROGRAMS BECAUSE THEY ARE UNABLE TO PROFIT FROM INSTRUCTION IN A NORMAL SCHOOL SETTING, WHERE THEY MAKE IT DIFFICULT FOR OTHER CHILDREN TO RECEIVE INSTRUCTION." [2]

So if you were the kind of kid who couldn't be controlled or who proved to be disruptive -- or because of cultural misunderstandings or fear based prejudices on the part of frustrated teachers and administrators -- you were sent to a 600 school. First, there would have likely been a series of beatings you received in school and at home because the standard mode of therapy for anyone who didn't conform, couldn't pay attention or function without disruptive outbursts was public humiliation, beatings and then suspension. If that failed, you were jailed in a 600 school. While they claimed that their intent was to eventually reintegrate you if possible, the few students I knew of whom had vanished into this realm never returned.

In elementary school, I saw the toughest kid in the neighborhood's younger brother once scale the thirty foot chain link fence that housed the recessed courtyard of our school. The dean and several teachers eventually talked him down. I asked him why he had done it, and he simply shrugged, saying, "I wanted to know what it felt like." He had hung backwards off the fence, releasing one hand, letting his head drop until it nearly pointed straight down at the concrete 30 feet below him. They sent him to a 600 school after the incident.

Later in life, I met someone who'd graduated from a 600 school, and he calmly told me that it hadn't been a bad experience at all -- that the rumors of what things were like for students had been greatly exaggerated. He'd actually benefited from the experience. Of course, at the time we were engaged in juvenile delinquent street activities together, and while I had been a stellar student in school, I felt him "weak" when it came to running the streets. Perhaps the school had done something for him after all. It had taught him through consequences the costs of not conforming.

In 1961, my sister, Veronica, had slipped past the intake interview in elementary school, perhaps because in those days her daydreaming could take on passive qualities; however, on the first day of school when the schoolyard whistle was blown and she remained the only person in motion, the jig was up. The sight of her dashing across a yard filled with still-as-statue students while she spoke to her fingers in a made up language, giggling insanely, was enough to scare many of the students to death -- at least those who didn't laugh at her. My mother was called, Veronica got picked up, and that morning in the principal's office, she was simply told, "Your daughter requires the kind of care we can't offer here." That was that.

Veronica ended up a private school for disturbed children that cost a small fortune. Each morning, Veronica would be shuttled away to a "special" location in that stigmatic yellow mini "cheese bus". The school's owner claimed that one of the local assemblymen had graduated from the place. It was a hellhole that required students to scrub floors on their hands and knees and clean the insides of toilets – all for several thousand dollars of your 1960's money. My parents clung onto to the fantasy that Veronica would one day get well.

Years passed and some more palatable public services became available to my family. At first, Veronica was able to find a free education by taking two city buses on her own; eventually she was able to walk to the local school, which had a lockdown community of mental defectives like herself all bunched together in several asylum-like rooms. The SPED students were kept remotely separate, which seemed to further stigmatize them. Sometimes they could be seen moving from the Annex to the main building for lunch or gym strung together in a line literally by string. If students from the main building were present, these mental defectives were heckled and jeered at; sometimes, someone even threw something at them, perhaps a remnant of their free lunch. I witnessed my sister in this prison like line being heckled, some students hurling remnants of their uneaten lunch at the group. I felt pained and ashamed and turned away for a moment. Then I looked back. First out of guilt. Then at how angry I had felt: afraid that my sister would be injured as someone threw most of an apple at the group; I was helpless to protect her.

    Veronica also had additional support services available to her, psychiatrists who experimented on her with a variety of medications always relevant to their new diagnoses -- pet theories on what was wrong with her: Veronica was mentally retarded and emotionally disturbed; she was also schizophrenic. My family had won the trifecta of mental illnesses. Later on, she'd be further diagnosed as autistic. Each new diagnosis required medication being piled upon medication, with her newly medicated condition then diagnosed and treated with more medications, prescribed by doctors who never communicated with one another. At the end of it all, she was nearly a vegetable. And that got diagnosed to. And medicated – until she ended up not once, but twice in a coma with no oxygen going to her brain for more than 15 minutes and then 20 minutes, respectively. And the condition in which she came out of that coma got diagnosed and medicated -- until the life in her simply left.

    In this Brooklyn elementary school where I received my first formal education – the one that could not help my sister a few years before I had entered -- I watched the one male teacher, who was also the dean, physically pick up a student and bounce said student off a stone wall multiple times – all under the direction of the principal, Mrs. Driscoll. Her name looked close enough to the word "discipline" to become synonymous with it in my child's mind.

    The student, now in a semiconscious state, was allowed to return to class in a more receptive condition. If you received a beating in school, you were certain to get another when you got home. And any kid who wanted to work, could, just as long as he could find someone to hire him. In my Brooklyn neighborhood, many families were forced to send their children to work, either at a family owned business or any local establishment that was willing to pay. One of our students, Johnny, worked with a plumber carrying radiators. He eventually developed legs like two tree stumps and a reputation for knocking out men -- although he was only in the 6th grade.

As I progressed through this institution of learning, the 6th grade was eliminated. And a brand new Intermediate school opened up to usher in the now volatile population of sixth, seventh, and eighth graders. The place was complete chaos compared to my elementary school. I once watched a student physically fight a teacher, while I rooted for the student. Fortunately, I tested gifted that year for the second time and entered an accelerated program at another, better run, though still chaotic, JHS.

Rules changed. By the time I entered teaching nearly 20 years later, teachers could no longer "discipline" students by using physical force -- at least in NYC. Nearly 15 years before, serious child abuse laws had been enacted, and now newer labor laws were stringently enforced, making it harder for younger kids to work. Our society had become enlightened.

When I entered the classroom, teachers were expected to tolerate the verbal and under certain conditions as laid out in their IEPs (Individual Education Plans), physical abuse from some students. At least that's what I have been told by several different special ed teachers. Harassment against teachers by students has, in general, become much more prevalent. [3,4,5]

Neither the approach of being physically brutal and psychologically harsh, nor the overprotectiveness of our youth to the point that we unrealistically insulate them from their own consequences -- the very means by which most of us have learned our life lessons -- works. Perhaps we might benefit from a different kind of education, one that taught us more about ourselves, as CPE had taught its students.

Currently, with three and four year olds being mandated to attend pre-k and school days and years being extended, much of education feel as if it's little more than a prolonged indoctrination into our society, leaving students with little or no marketable skills. [6,7]

Education fails to fully take into account a student's life situation, capabilities, and interests. The use of uniform standards for literacy and numeracy across the country as the benchmark by which we measure the effectiveness of education ignores at least five other intelligences. (Howard Gardner effectively made the case for multiple intelligences: linguistic, logical, spatial, body kinesthetic, musical, inter and intrapersonal.) Our present approach to education may be somewhat palatable for about half of all students, with an additional 25% learning to struggle through it. The remaining 25% dropout. [8,9,10] Those who do graduate from high school but fail to go on to earn additional credentials end up under employed. [11]

Without additional education after high school, students cannot reasonably expect to earn a livable wage: if this were the only consequence of our current educational system, it would be tragic enough. Unfortunately, it's what we do to some of the most vulnerable amongst us, perhaps some of the most creative and sensitive -- the ones who see the world differently and can't let go of their own inner vision -- is most heartbreaking.

In the most extreme cases, if you as a student fail to fit in -- because that's what most public education is teaching you -- we as teachers, administrators, social workers, school psychiatrists, etc… are obliged to do everything we can to force your round peg through a not quite suitable hole -- even if it means demonizing you or institutionalizing you.

I've heard of our 'mandatory" education referred to as a 14 year prison term. Our system mandates that anyone who can't keep up should eventually be discarded in some form or other. Sometimes we do it through labelling: You're a "dropout" or "learning disabled" or "attention deficit hyperactivity disorder" -- labels which too often translate into "failure," "limited," and "unable to learn". Those who do drop out -- or who are unable to negotiate through a "higher education" -- don't easily get jobs, not ones that pay a livable wage. [12]

Of particular concern is the inordinate number of black and hispanic students that have been classified as "Special Ed," a designation once hard to come by and severely limited in scope. [13] By misdiagnosing students as "Special Ed," we not only do them a disservice, but we also limit the effectiveness of those services available to students who really need them. And some students do need them, will benefit from the diagnosis and additional support and treatment. The highest failure rate in NYC is of black and hispanic students; the lowest percentage of students who complete a four year college degree is from the same bucket. [14] When you consider that there is a disproportionate number of blacks and hispanics populating this country's penal institutions, these statistics appear to be connected.

Some people have used these numbers to make a case for the existence of institutional racism.

"Racism" of this magnitude pervading both educational and justice systems is indicative of something even greater and perhaps more insidious: I'll argue that what we call "racism" because of its impact on those who are targeted is actually depersonalization. At its core, it's fear and self-hatred directed at others. Dehumanization lies at the root of all our evils.

In order to level the playing field in a true sense, we all need a different sort of education, one that will teach us that our own biases -- and we all have them -- are often buried beneath layers of good intentions, cleverly hidden from ourselves. What if part of becoming a teacher, a police officer, a corrections officer, etc... required a deep and thorough "education" which taught us how to understand ourselves in a non-judgmental way. What if we were taught compassion first and foremost?

What if our education thoroughly examined, without accusation, the notion that a disproportionate number of any group failing socially is the result of both intentional and unintentional social targeting of that group from multiple vantage points. White people don't accidentally think of people of color differently; that sort of thinking pervades educational systems, media and news outlets including film and advertising, as well as justice systems.

It is subtly woven into the fabric of our deeper and more hidden selves, and it colors our perceptions and often unknowingly dictates our responses: demonization of the "unsafe other" as Tara Brach calls it. It is a fear based, lashing out and shutting down of our thinking brains: a completely ineffective method of protecting ourselves against a perceived threat, against what we fear on a primal level, which exists, ironically, in ourselves -- not outside. So it's a losing paradigm: I cannot assuage my fears by battling imagined threats outside of me when those demons live inside and control my responses in ways I cannot even fathom.

Consider that people of color have long ago "learned" to think of themselves differently, have accustomed themselves to the onslaught of institutional dehumanization. Ask yourself: Are we the human race? Or are we separate and unequal? Either we're all cut from the same divine cloth or we're not. What if education gently and non-judgmentally revealed this in a way where we might compassionately begin to change and heal?

In 2006, I attended a conference run by the superintendent of our district where he openly and somewhat sardonically admitted that as a child, he had been diagnosed as "special ed." He told us that he had been bored and as a result acted out mischievously in class. Being black in a school populated by white teachers and a white administration, he had been diagnosed as having behavioral problems and a learning disability. His mother fought the diagnosis and eventually won.

In the second grade, my oldest son had been suspected of suffering from ADHD by a teacher of two years experience because of his behavior in her classroom. She insisted that we have him diagnosed "for his own good." At the time, his mother, Cuban, and I were in the midst of a divorce but paused long enough to bond together over this one issue: we moved Nick to another school where the next year he tested in the 90 percentile in both reading and math across the entire city. We later learned that Nick's former teacher had herself just emerged from a divorce, and that her issues had colored her perspective.

The idea that a wholly unqualified person or persons can redirect your child's life, perhaps because of his own ignorance or issues, placing it on a tragic trajectory, is frightening. Yet, that's the kind of damage an inexperienced, frustrated or "issue laden" educator can easily do in a system not designed to assess and address the needs of its most vulnerable, a system run by individuals who haven't been educated to watch out for how their own needs drive them. And teachers, like so many other professionals, come to their profession "issue laden", unaware that they are working out their own personal mythologies through their work and in the process, they sometimes intentionally, sometimes unintentionally, harm those they have been charged with helping and protecting.

How can you change a system from within when those who are charged with that responsibility have likely been partially blinded by that very system? Our fourteen years of mandatory and uniform education may actually be dangerous. Maybe it should come with a warning like the ones on medications:

"Warning: If you are black, hispanic, female, LGBTQIA+ or a member of any marginalized group (subject to the least favorite flavor of the month rule), your education may be substandard providing you don't have sufficient income to offset the fundamental biases and the resulting harm you will incur through the continued use of this system. Prolonged use of this system may result in feelings of inferiority, inadequacy or self-hatred. You may tend to expect less of yourself and for yourself, experiencing bouts of anger, frustration and/or depression as a result of the inequitable and inhumane treatment you sometimes receive. Explosions of rage may occur. On a core level, you may scream out, 'WHY CAN'T YOU SEE THE PERSON THAT I AM?" This may likely be diagnosed and treated. All attempts at correcting these biases are likely to be met with expressions of incredulity and anger by the proprietors of the system. Prolonged overtures of frustration, outrage, defiance, and/or disgust on your part towards the administrators of this system may result in institutional blowback. In some cases, excessive resistance to the breaking of your spirit has resulted in institutionalization, demonization, and/or death."

There is simply something inherently wrong with a systematized form of education that offers what is now 14 years of fairly uniform curriculum to the entire population in order to achieve basic competencies before any meaningful form of specialization can begin. There is absolutely no basic level of literacy or numeracy that requires 14 years to impart -- unless the purpose of such a lengthy education is also to indoctrinate children into a specific mindset that won't allow them to question whether or their current society is a healthy one worth participating in.

Many students emerge fourteen years later with still no clue as to what they want to do with their lives or how they can earn a meaningful living, finding themselves having to pursue four to seven additional years of education. It's a prison sentence. Does anyone really want to argue that you can't produce a minimally competent medical professional in 14 years providing you completely redesigned how education works?

We live in a world that has monopolized education, medicine, and justice by institutionalizing these things as if they are marketed commodities that one is forced to purchase -- only our public institutions offer one kind of education, one kind of medical treatment, one kind of justice -- so unless you possess the resources to obtain better, you'll likely suffer.

Perhaps our entire approach is just wrong. We've been

"educated" to deal with the inequality of racism rather than address its root cause; we'd rather kill the cancer than prevent the conditions that create it; we believe in incarcerating the criminal rather than nurturing and educating the child. Why do we prefer to spend two and three times more money to incarcerate a teenager than we spend to educate that same teenager.[15] Doesn't it mean anything that the recidivism rate for incarcerated teens still hovers around 80%?[16] To make matters worse, those who have greater means are able to purchase better educations, finer medical treatment, and more palatable forms of justice from the public institutions which are supposed to serve all of us equally.

As a teacher, you ask yourself how do I educate a child who doesn't want to learn what I'm required to teach knowing if that child doesn't achieve the highest level of education attainable, his options will be greatly limited -- while I work in a school of limited means and am constrained by a system that may not have this child's best interest at heart? How do I teach someone who may have come to believe that his failure to learn and excel in required areas is indicative of his innate inferiority? Or the result of a system that is designed to work against him? Or that justice doesn't exist for people who look like him?

I felt compelled to teach something the child could succeed at -- something I witnessed my colleagues do time and again -- something outside of the curricula. And through teaching this other thing, I worked toward teaching the essentials which lie behind the curricula requirements: literacy, numeracy, higher order thinking, etc....

I've always felt obligated to tell my students that I believed we live in a world, which because of their race, their color, their economics, required them to forge through education an accredited key or else they were not likely to open the door to an economically viable existence.

I was sitting across the table from my 14 year old son a year after I had retired, and he said to me, "Dad, you know what they should do with schools?"

I looked up at this kid who had been an honor student for years, was going to a private high school on a partial scholarship and who had made his freshman baseball team and just said, "Go on."

"Companies should test you. And depending on how you do, set up programs to educate you so that you're trained to do work for them that you'd be good at. This way, when you get out of school, you know you'll have a job that you can do and that you might enjoy. All this other stuff school insists you learn seems like a huge waste of time."

"What about art and music?"

"They could teach you that stuff if they wouldn't act like it was so important -- unless it was something you were good at and wanted to do. Why force the rest of us to learn things we're not good at and that we will never use in our lives. It's like we're being punished." Some of the charter schools had already begun moving down roads in that direction. His statement that "learning useless stuff feeling like punishment" had been said to me by students from every single class I had ever taught. Why wasn't learning more enjoyable? Weren't we capable of doing that?

What would be so difficult about instituting different kinds of education where groups of students who wanted to study art, music, technology, carpentry, mechanics, plumbing, electricity, masonry, cosmetology, medicine, astronomy, etc... simply entered specialized schools -- instead of a traditional high school -- where they were guaranteed internships and eventual employment in fields where they both showed interest and promise.

What if our society didn't punish our children for not having a college education by forcing them into low wage jobs that didn't allow them to pay rent or support a family in a dignified manner? That might force university tuitions to drop for those student who did want to pursue that trajectory. At the same time, having alternative forms of education whose successful completion provided respectable employment with a living wage could also insulate our children against illegal and dangerous lifestyles -- especially if the payoffs began with paid internships after a year or two of "higher schooling", instead of having to wait for the additional eight years one takes to finish both high school and college, amounting to a total of 18 years of formalized schooling.

Do we not see that the unfair way in which we educate our poor, our minorities, and our social "outcasts", whomever these might be at the time, helps to create the criminality that currently plagues our inner cities? And would it be a surprise to anyone to discover that the disenfranchisement of individuals from society is the direct result, at least in part, of a poorly designed educational system, inadequate psychological and medical interventions, and marginalizing employment cultures -- not to mention the multitude of discriminatory policies and practices we don't even acknowledge are subtly interwoven into the fabric of all our social systems. We perpetuate the abject poverty that we despise through the fearful ways we attempt to insulate ourselves against it. And out of this poverty -- and the contempt and fear we show towards those who have been born of it or who have been devastated by it -- the evils of our world abound.

[1] *"600" Schools, Yesterday, Today and Tomorrow*, ERIC, 2-1-1965

[2] *Dealing with Violent Behavior*, NEA 6-1-2011

[3] *When Educators are Assulted*, NEA, 3-1-2011

[4] *Violence Against Teachers - An Overlooked Crises?* NEA, 2-19-2013

[5] *Thirteen Reasons Why America's High Schools are Creating Another Lost Generation*, Zero Hedge, 5-23-2017

[6] *Why High School Students Need More Than College Prep*, NPR, 7-10-2016

[7] *Education Department Releases 2015 High School Graduation Rates*, New York State Education Dept., 6-2-2016

[8] *Public High School Graduation Rates*, WNYC, 6-2-2016

[9] *New York City High School Dropouts*, You Are Here, 6-2-2015

[10] *It's Nearly Impossible To Make A Livable Wage Without A College Education*, Business Insider, 11-1-2011

[11] *Special Education and the Mis-education of African American Children*, The Association of Black Psychologists, 2-13-2012

[12] *U.S. Education: Still Separate and Unequal*, US News, 1-28-2015

[13] *Portrayal of Minorities in Film and Media*, Stanford, 6-2-2016

[14] *Racial Psychology: Why Do Black People Want to be White?* New Observer, 6-2-2016

[15] *Long-Term Juvenile Incarceration Fails to Decrease Reoffending*, Center on Juvenile and Criminal Justice, 5-3-2012

[16] *In A Shocking Twist, Wealth Can Buy You Justice*, Reverb Press, 2015

Chapter Ten

Second Chances

I am drinking at a bar. Hours before I had plenty of money, and I had been held by the expectation that a group of people from work, people whose company I enjoy, would join me. Now, just back from a cocaine run, I'm looking at nearly every loser in the school drinking off my money -- money that I left on the bar while I disappeared to buy drugs.

    I pull most of my remaining cash off the bar and leave, saying next to nothing. Every fiber in my being resists acknowledging the scathing truth people know about me, that exposes itself against my will: I am damaged, unfit for the company of others; trouble has always followed me wherever I go.

~

For nine years, I worked in an alternative high school in Bushwick Brooklyn. It probably was one of the best kept secrets in an otherwise deteriorating neighborhood. Our school, which housed around 280 students when full, generally serviced closer to 140 students throughout the school year. What that created for the teachers were classes with around 15 students, relaxed interactions, time for individual attention, and a safe learning environment that encouraged second chances.

It was the early 90's. As it was explained to me by one of the guidance counselors, all we had to do was meet register by October 31st to receive full funding. If on November 1st, we discharged half the school, we still kept the money. We were a state funded program contained in a city funded school, so we drew monies from both buckets. We housed a small GED program, maybe 60 students on register, who came to class for two hours each morning, sometimes remaining the rest of the day, which ended at 12:40 with lunch and then dismissal. Our entire teaching day ran straight through from 9:00 am until 12:40 with no breaks. The remaining two hours we were on our own.

"So what do we do from 12:40 until 2:40?"

"You're kidding, right?"

"No, seriously."

"Hide." I was told by the veteran teacher I'd seen changing the answers on the state Math test that same year.

These were heavy drinking years, and while I frequently got very drunk and regularly came to work reeking of last night's or even that morning's booze, I never once got in trouble for it. The culture was different. Both guidance counselors kept bottles of whiskey in their office, and the college advisor always had a bottle handy -- one you could slip a shot from anytime you needed. Alcohol was still permitted inside of city schools.

I even got drunk once on the job, though it was a no-student contact day. I simply went across the street to the Bodega with Johnny, my Vietnam Vet buddy, and we each drank a six pack at ten in the morning. Then I walked around the building announcing to everyone who would listen how drunk I was and how good I felt. I got sent home, but no letter was put in my file. Things were about to change.

Flo taught literacy to students with special needs. Her room sat just beyond the lunchroom but before the set of double doors that separated us from the JHS, which housed our entire site, and it contained several thousand books, all meticulously ordered by reading level and identifiable literacy needs. When one of our colleagues, an English teacher named Timothy, rose to the ranks of Center

Administrator, he got it in his head that Flo, now a 27 year veteran but originally a dental hygienist by profession, couldn't teach.

"What do you think of Flo as a teacher?" he asked me only a week after he'd taken over.

"She seems to do well with the students. They're very comfortable with her."

"Have you ever observed her teaching?"

"No." At that point, I hadn't observed any of my colleagues.

"I'm not sure she knows what she's doing."

"Really. Hasn't she been teaching for over 25 years?"

"That's my point. Did you know she used to be a dental hygienist?"

"No. Is that a bad thing?"

"Well, you don't exactly have to be a rocket scientist to clean teeth."

"Are you saying that you think she's dumb?"

"Well, yeah."

Flo spoke to me about Timothy. "Timothy keeps coming into my room."

"What do you think that's about?"

"I don't know. I get the impression he doesn't think that I know how to teach."

"Why?"

"He keeps telling me to do things in ways I know wouldn't work with these students. Does he understand that they're Special Education students?"

Timothy called me aside on another day. He seemed agitated. "You speak with Flo. What's your impression of her?"

"As a person?"

"Well, yes."

"She's reads people well. She knows the students she works with, cares about them, and works hard with them."

"Yeah, but she speaks to them as if they were children. Did you know that she has a common branch license?"

"Timothy, I don't even know what a common branch license is."

"It's for teaching elementary school. I think that's what she should be doing."

"She's been doing this job for a lot of years now. I've never heard anyone complain about her. Besides, if she didn't know how to handle these particular students, why would we have hired her in the first place?"

"I don't know. They act like she's their mother. Maybe they like that. It doesn't necessarily mean that they're learning anything."

"These kids are largely Special Ed students. Maybe her gentle approach works."

"We need a Special Ed teacher for those students, not somebody who acts like their mother."

In September, Timothy hired a Special Education teacher, who appeared to be in need of help herself. It should be noted that Timothy is the person who sent me home for being drunk on the job. He also would later rehire me after I'd lost my job for abandonment of position due to excessive drinking. Teaching could be a very forgiving profession.

At our first staff meeting, and I do mean our first staff meeting, Lynn, the new SPED teacher, sat picking her nose. Part of Timothy's taking over as Center Administrator meant we no longer could run out the backdoor at 12:40.

About an hour into the meeting, Lynn absently lifted her left leg and part of her butt cheek off the seat to blow out one of the loudest farts I've ever heard. One of my colleagues fell to the floor laughing uncontrollably. Timothy asked him to leave the room as he was being disruptive.

Lynn took over Flo's classes and her classroom. The first thing she did was reorganize Flo's room. The term had just begun, and as is the case every September, we had four days alone as a staff before the students were permitted into the building.

I poked my head into what was now Lynn's room on day one. She had already pulled more than a thousand books off the shelves and out of the closets, piling them first on the chairs and desks, and eventually onto the floor.

"How you doing?"

"Just trying to get organized here. I can't seem to find any materials."

"You could ask Flo. She'd be glad to help you. I'm pretty sure she knows where everything is."

"That's the thing. *I need to know* where everything is."

"O-kay."

She continued for days, managing to move all the furniture to the four corners of the room with massive piles of books filling every other space.

This process, wherein Lynn had disassembled Flo's life's work over a four day period of time was witnessed by the entire staff. It became the hot topic of conversation.

"What is Lynn doing?"

"I don't know?"

"Why is she reorganizing everything? If there ever was one thing Flo was good at, it was organization."

"Yeah. Everything in that room was perfectly in place."

On day three, people started taking bets. "I don't see how she's ever going to finish. I mean, I just looked in there, and it's a bigger mess than it was just a few hours before."

And Flo lamented the whole painful process. "It's like I'm watching someone take apart my life."

In the end, with just one hour before students arrived, and after the staff collectively urged him to, Timothy poked his head in the door and said this to a drooling and over medicated Lynn who sat helplessly on the floor, a single book hanging from one limp hand. "Students are about to arrive. You need to get this room in order."

An hour later, every single book had been removed from the floor and housed away. The furniture had been put in place and it looked like a classroom -- only now none of the materials would ever be located again.

The next thing Lynn did was to order her own materials.

"We don't seem to have materials to address the learning needs of the students." New materials were ordered. And then she began discarding all of the materials that had made up Flo's class, garbage bags at a time.

Flo had her own problems. "Timothy's got me teaching regular English. I have a common branch licence. I don't know how to teach high school English. They hired me to work with students who had special literacy needs"

"Have you told him that?"

"Yes. He told me that this is a high school, not an elementary school." By the end of the year, Flo felt compelled to retired.

The last thing she said to me was, "Timothy's an idiot."

Before Lynn was fired, we marked the English Regents together. Arn, the head English teacher, ran the marking sessions which lasted all day for three straight days.

"Look, we have 80 exams here, that's 320 essays from students, many of whom can hardly read or write. Each exam has to be read twice. It's going to be long and painful, so let's be fair about this. We're going to split them up so that everyone marks the same number."

Nine hours into the first day, Arn looked down at his pile.

"What the fuck is this?" He looked over at Lynn. "You must have accidentally put some of your exams in my pile." Lynn tried to shake her head, but he began to separate them. "I had up through "P" which means all of these are yours." He moved 60 essays back into her pile.

We left that room exhausted. I still had 50 essays left to mark.

The next day Timothy spoke with me. "Did you see what time Lynn left yesterday?"

"Yeah, why? About 15 minutes after me."

"Had she finished marking her exams?"

"Not even close."

"Well, they're all done." A long silence. "That means you and I are going to have to remark all her exams."

"Why's that?"

"Because all her grades are random."

"So make her mark them."

"You really want to entrust the future of some of our students to her grading practices?"

"You hired her."

"She's put in all failing grades."

"Well, we're going to need help."

"Okay. I'll get you Flo."

"Flo?"

"Yeah. You have a problem working with her?"

"Not at all. I just thought that you didn't think too highly of her."

"Well, what choice do we have?"

Flo turned out to be a hard marker with an incredibly astute and critical eye. I began to tease her during the marking as she was my partner.

"Here you go, Chopper. Go get him."

"What are you talking about?"

"Fail the son of a bitch."

"You saying I'm marking too hard?"

"I think all of your observations are on point. How Timothy ever imagined you couldn't teach English is beyond me. You have a sharper eye for language than I have. However, if we mark this critically, none of them will pass."

"They don't deserve to pass writing like this."

"You're probably right, but do you really imagine that they'll get any better in another year when all they're thinking is 'I'm 20 now and still in high school'?"

"So what are you saying?"

"I'm saying to be as gentle and generous as your conscience allows."

"I thought I was."

We laughed so hard I could hardly breathe. I missed her every day after she left.

One of our teachers, Sylvia, took students away to Canada to work as junior counselors in her summer camp. Apparently, it turned out to be an abusive situation for the students who claimed they weren't even allowed to make phone calls to have their parents take them back home.

I spoke about it with Arn, the heroin addict English teacher who ran the writing lab. "It's the Gulag. Those kids are used for slave labor. They try to escape, but it's all the way up in Canada so they have no way to get home. They aren't even allowed to use the phone. I think she feeds them bread and water and locks them up at night. She's under investigation by the state department."

Another teacher, an older white male, spent his summers in a nudist camp. Each year prior to student contact day, he littered the desks with nude pictures of preteens.

"Why does Bill leave all these photocopies of nude underage girls around?"

"He makes my skin crawl." One of the female teachers said. "I can't even go in his room."

"Hey Bill?" I asked him one day. "What's up with the naked girls?"

"They're beautiful, aren't they?"

"They're a little young."

He smiled.

"Maybe you should put the material away before the students arrive."

~

We had a very successful writing center run by Arn. When the Principal took complete credit for all his accomplishments, accepting an award for the successes of the school's writing lab, Arn left. Arn had been a powerful teacher, taking genuine interest in his students and taking the time to collaboratively create a strategy for passing the state writing exam by breaking down the entire exam into each of the tasks a student had to know in order to tackle the three writing components. He spent months with student tutors developing and then refining the strategy. It became the model I used to teach students how to pass that exam.

I used the approach, though slightly modified, after Arn left, trying it out on my literacy class which I taught for two hours a day each morning, and seven out of the ten students in the class passed the exam even though they read on a third and fourth grade level.

The idea that certain skills which we as literate people take for granted are actually comprised of many mini skills, some of which less than literate people may have not yet mastered became the model that helped me to create literacy strategies: What is it that this student isn't getting? What step is he missing? It often ended up being something that I considered so small as to not consider at all. Teaching was always a learning process for me, and I told my students that our job is to discover how you learn as individuals and then to help you use that information so that you can succeed at whatever it is you want. Sometimes, that involved discovering what pieces to the puzzle were missing and to then help the students create those pieces for themselves.

Another teacher, Clara, had gotten into the habit of arriving just minutes before nine o'clock and the start of her first period class. Although she was Jewish, she spoke spanish fluently, and the students loved her and excelled in her class. When Timothy took over, he came after her every single day about her latenesses. At the end of the year, she felt compelled to leave too.

    I went through a divorce that year, moved into the neighborhood with my 23 year old girlfriend, being 35 at the time myself. My drinking got out of control, and she left during an ugly fight. I only had the ugly fights when I wasn't drinking. When I drank, I found myself peaceful, but I never wanted to stop, never wanted to live as the person I was when I wasn't drinking.

    Shame and self-hatred can echo through a person in powerful and deafening waves that, unless you've experienced them, no one can explain them to you. Just divorced and now with my younger girlfriend leaving me, I felt like dying in order to hide from the scrutiny of others. People take their own lives rather than live within the depths of that shame.

    I eventually went into my first inpatient treatment program. The job granted me a medical sabbatical and I was paid 60% of my salary while I struggled to get well. I felt fragile enough to break. After I told the doctor doing intake that I could never face my colleagues again, he told me that he was in recovery too. I asked him how he managed to face his colleagues after what he'd done. He told me that it wasn't easy but he simply didn't have a choice. I held on to that: if a doctor could drink himself out of his job and come back from that kind of shame, then maybe I could find the courage too.

    The school I worked for was changing. New levels of accountability were being introduced. A year later, I returned, and eight months later, I drank again. I held onto what the wizened woman who had reprocessed me into my position had said, "They helped you this time. It's none of anyone's business what you went through. But if you mess up again, you on your own."

    Feeling as if there was no hope for me, I turned on the gas in the apartment. The walls faded. I saw a line of shadowy figures many deep encircling me at the perimeter of what were once the walls of my apartment. As the beer nearly slipped from my hand, the phone rang and I decided to answer it. I got my second chance.

    I still went homeless, abandoning my apartment and then living in a hotel upstate where I drank five bottles of wine a day for six weeks, before entering the Brooklyn VA hospital for 22 days and finally winding up in a therapeutic community for 10 months where

I eventually returned to teaching, working for Timothy in one of his other schools, while still living in the lockdown community and on public assistance. It was painfully humbling.

The thing about second chances is we all really need them, yet we live in a world that has become increasingly unforgiving. I worked in an imperfect school with imperfect people. Granted, some of them should have never been allowed in a classroom. Perhaps at times I should have been considered one of those. Yet, lives changed in that school. Students found hope, went on to college, to the military, to careers, to raise families and find sanctuary in their own well-beings. Still, the administrators who ran that school and the organizations that monitored them were filled by human beings who increasingly lacked the very compassion that they expected those employed by them to display on a daily basis.

This paradox of ideals where employees are treated one way by the organization they work for while being expected to exhibit a diametrically opposed set of attitudes towards those they service has become the hallmark of the service industry. The results have been splashed across the headlines of papers for the past decade: from workers in hospital emergency rooms walking by while patients lay dying on the floor, to police officers fatally shooting members of the community they've sworn to protect and serve. If you asked an aide why she passed a man who lay their dying and did nothing, she'd tell you that I have 20 other patients to attend to, that Mr. Smith needs his insulin shot and I got to go change Mrs. Jones' bedpan and I've been on a 16 hour shift without a break and I gotta pee. Besides, it ain't my job." And if you asked the cop who kicked in the door of an apartment, chasing after an adolescent who had been selling marijuana and then shot the unarmed boy dead in front of his grandmother while the young man attempted to flush the weed down the toilet, he'd tell you, "I was chasing a bad guy who resisted arrest. I caught him trying to destroy evidence. He wasn't going to get away with that." When the pressures of the job overshadow our own humanity, then we become inhumane.

We attempt to administer justice and equality in our society as if they were commodities we can distribute. We punish those who fail to properly administer this "justice" and "equality", never connecting the increasingly inhumane way in which we treat each other, even when we work with the same goals in mind, with the horrific acts that too many of us consequently commit. An education system that fails to raise the consciousness of its students and ultimately, the society it's supposed to serve, fails all of us.

Why doesn't education teach us about ourselves in a meaningful way? Why don't we learn about how our minds work and the connection between self-care, balance, and happiness? Why don't we have mindfulness, loving kindness, and forgiveness practices infused into our curricula so that after 14 years of education it resonates throughout our being? At the very least, we'd understand what it takes to be happy. On the darker side, shouldn't we understand what drives us to be less than noble?

Consider that the schools across this country are run by flawed individuals as all eight schools that I taught in were. Consider that these struggling souls, despite their sometimes flaring dysfunctions, would like to serve the greater good -- even if it is for their own selfish purposes or out of less than healthy needs. What is this greater good? Is it pushing the nearly illiterate on to higher levels of education where many will be made to feel increasingly inadequate, struggling souls who may or may not escape with a set of credentials that on paper indicate levels of competency that they indeed do not possess? Or is it to raise social awareness while preparing people to live in a future not yet fully realized with the hope that they will meaningfully contribute to both their generation and the next?

As a society, we simply aren't conscious on a level where we're able to decide what our true purpose should be so we aren't in a position to backward design our institutions. We can't redesign our institutions without deeply and non-judgmentally understanding and accepting ourselves.

Right now, whatever else you might think of education, a teacher's job is to help his students uncover and realize their own potential. Anyone who believes that teaching is about learning skills doesn't understand what teachers are up against. It's like saying that drug addiction is a law enforcement issue. I heard a police officer in a documentary about drug addiction state that, "We are facing a community crisis, and if we don't handle it as such, we run the risk of losing an entire generation." With education, we are disabling a generation by failing to raise them to be responsible, compassionate, open-minded, and socially conscious individuals who can earn a livable wage with a reasonable effort in a humane time frame. These are complex problems: how do we, as imperfect beings who have been tainted by an antiquated and prejudicial system of formalized education that more often limits than frees, create an environment that awakens the truth within this up and coming generation? Shouldn't we reveal our humanity? Shouldn't we acknowledge our flaws and limitations rather than pretend to be authorities of integrity; shouldn't we model a livable humanity?

Part of that unforgiving quality we too often use against one another is reflected in how specialized we've become. There's an irony to this "specialization", this over administration of our world in that it often creates the opposite of what it was originally designed to do.

After I retired, I volunteered at the VA hospital. There I rediscovered that it doesn't matter if you're good at something, you often can't get a job doing it without the proper credentials, this set of specific qualifications that involve formalized training, passing exams, and earning certifications. The opposite is also true. You don't have to be particularly good at a thing as long as you have the credentials to qualify you for the job. This is destructive to the human spirit. I saw people who weren't even literate in English, who couldn't speak or write fluently, working as receptionists and beyond while I couldn't successfully negotiate the application process.

I discovered that my 20 years of schooling -- thirty three graduate credits above my Masters Degree -- my 15 years of experience working with computers, networking, troubleshooting, my eight years of database work, and my 22 years as a classroom teacher, where I also spent time helping to train other teachers -- none of this, as well as all of it combined, qualified me to do anything. I couldn't even teach any longer: I no longer had the current qualifications!

What's wrong with an Educational system where 14 years of education doesn't qualify a person for employment beyond minimum wage? What's wrong with a system that is so focused, yet frustratingly futile at times, that four additional years (a university degree) just gains a person entrance into the job market above minimum wage -- but with this caveat: you need at least two years experience before most employees are willing to pay for your qualifications! So we're talking 20 years of education now before you can begin to earn a liveable wage. And then you're cornered into a specific type of career unless you're willing to gain additional education, certifications, and experience.

There's an unforgiving quality about this mentality -- especially when you consider how flawed we are as human beings, how so many of us are simply hanging on. This bureaucratic structure says that unless you can dedicate yourself for a 20 year period of time, minimally, you may not amount to anything in this life. In effect, many are denied even a fair first chance.

When I think about the people I've taught with, how deeply flawed so many of them were, yet how effective and caring they could be as classroom teachers, as counselors, as mentors, and then I juxtapose that with how so many of them left the profession, were forced into early retirements or out of teaching completely because they caved under the ever changing and mounting demands placed on them or they simply couldn't work the job and continue to satisfy the numerous and constantly changing certifications required by a profession, I'm saddened. The ways in which we were treated as professionals seemed at times diametrically opposed to the love and concern that our profession demanded we dole out to the children placed in our care. At other times, we were simply allowed to get away with far too much. And maybe, many simply needed more help and support from ourselves, each other and the community at large that we might in the end better serve.

~

I have no money, am out of alcohol and cocaine, and have no way of making it back home to get more cash. It is the middle of the night and I want it to be an endless night where I can hide forever in its darkened womb, but I know daylight will come, and by the time I make it back home to borrow money back from my girl only to return to the gambling machine in the back of the bodega, it will nearly be four. I will have to leave soon or people, responsible people, will see me in the condition that I am in. I am almost numb, can barely speak or stand, but if I could just push it a bit further, I'd reach the place where I don't care. And then I'd be alright. For a while anyway. Only I never really reach that place. Instead, I pass straight through it and blackout. I wake up on a dirty bed in a sleazy hotel. I am alone. I have no money, don't know how to get home and want to cry.

Chapter Eleven

Measure This

I*'m playing in the sand on the beach, watching waves break against the shore. My brother and sisters are there with me so it is a joyful time. I watch my older brother struggle past the breaking waves, but when I try to follow, I only get pushed back or knocked down. He comes and helps me beyond the breaking point where we now can jump the waves together.*

It is Saturday morning and I am up before dawn, ready to ride on the back of my brother's bicycle. I stand shivering in the cold, holding the bike up against the wind while he locks the door. I brave the weather as I will get to race along the road through Prospect Park, as headlights sometimes wipe away the night. Night. The world is a different place full of mystery and delight. My dreams hide here. My nightmares live and breed here though only when I am alone.

Yet, as we soar down the long hill, avenue after avenue, speeding along, just catching the lights, and making it home moments before dawn breaks, I somehow outrun the living dread which has haunted me even at this early age. I will spend much of the rest of my life, sometimes outrunning them, sometimes being overrun by them. I will recount these times to my brother before he dies, and he will remember them, as he remembers being homeless for nearly two years. We will talk about how he and I were homeless at the same time only neither of us knew it as he was in Florida and I in New York. Our sister was in a coma only months before. We wondered at the coincidence. "Could forces beyond our understanding be at work here?" Perhaps these same forces direct all of our lives, and what we view as human tragedy is simply the path we must follow to find our way back home.

~

After years of working for the Board of Education, I learned there were people, select individuals, whom I could contact that knew how to get things done. They'd managed to work in a particular department for 10, 15, even 20 years, and often they had responsible contacts in other departments. When I needed help, I'd simply call one of these people, who, over time I'd developed a relationship with. If that person couldn't help me with my problem, he'd go out of his way to find someone who could.

If I wanted to order a server for my computer lab, one which wasn't approved by the DOE, I could call someone down at the Board -- someone I'd grown to trust over the years -- who could take me through the process, steering me clear of any paperwork pitfalls that I might encounter, sometimes even recommending something better. If I needed to translate a transcript from the Dominican Republic or Mexico, I could make a phone call and somebody would know someone who could help. I liked these people, and I had grown to trust them, and they enjoyed doing their jobs well, even though I'd never met most of them face-to-face.

Once, a guy I'd call for help with ATS (Automate the Schools, a system of biographical data), noted that I didn't sound like myself, and he asked me about it.

"Paul, I'm sick."

"What's wrong?"

"Damn cold. Every year, turns into some kind of bronchial thing and then I'm sick on and off until April."

"You're kidding."

"No. My students give it to me and then I bring it home. It goes around the house, and when everyone gets better, I pick up another form of it from a different student."

"You take vitamins?"

"No."

"Tell you what you're going to do. Pick up some vitamin D. Say 5000 units.

Throw in a couple of C's. It'll knock it right out of you in a couple of days."

That was the first year in 20 plus that I didn't find myself sick from November through March. Paul died of a massive heart attack in China on his honeymoon right after he retired, and although I never met him in person, I felt as if I'd lost a dear friend.

When Mayor Mike Bloomberg took over for 12 years, instituting what he referred to as the business model, it resulted in the destruction of much of the NYCDOE's institutional memory. Over time, it became increasingly difficult to call an office and speak to someone you knew or for that matter, someone who knew what he was doing. Everyone had left: departments had been reorganized, people retrained, promoted, fired or retired. Had this happened only once, personal relationships between human beings at schools and district or central offices that had taken years to develop may have survived, but because this type of reorganization and consolidation appeared to be organic to the Bloomberg business model, these multiple downsizings and reorganizations had, instead, left us alone.

The human side to this story sounds something like this: seven years into my teaching career, I received a letter from the then Board of Education in late August telling me that I was having my teaching license pulled at the end of September for failure to complete my Masters Degree. When I went down to the office which had sent the letter, I spoke to a woman who told me that because they were revoking my permanent license as of September 30th, I would be allowed to teach until June that year. If I didn't obtain my Masters by June, I would be fired. She hinted that had I not completely finished but shown some progress, leniency might be possible. This was the old Board. I talked with a person who had the power to allow me to continue, who actually encouraged me to do the right thing. I had finished the necessary coursework years ago, but I simply refused to do the work for my thesis, figuring they'd never catch up with me.

That year, I contracted hepatitis, got a leave of absence in November and by the time I returned in February, I had nearly completed my Masters, which I finished by May. I saved my license and would be able to teach until my retirement 20 years later. When I got the good news in the form of a letter from the Board, I bought a bouquet of roses and decided to surprise the woman who had been so kind to me and had extended my teaching life. When I walked into her office and handed her the flowers, I discovered that I had walked in on her retirement party.

The new Department of Education sent a similar letter out to a colleague of mine 12 years later. Somehow, he'd managed to remain below radar for that long. And they simply fired him. It took him three years to get rehired as a paraprofessional -- not as a teacher any longer -- and while he was able to work until retirement, his present pension plus social security is close to two thousand dollars a month less than my pension alone -- even though we had started teaching at the exact same time -- the result of those lost years combined with his being forced to change job titles. And he had been forced to cash in his secondary pension account during those three years when he didn't work for the NYDOE. That became the new Department of Education.

When the DOE started changing systems, reshuffling people, and introducing endless levels of accountability, they became more demanding, feeling the right to hold people to a level of accountability that they themselves could never meet.

"No one seems to know what he's doing any more. Everyone's new," was the lamentable sentiment we often shared in the staff lounge. "I can't find anyone to help me with these new systems they want me to use. The people I do speak with don't seem to know any more than I do. And sometimes they just give me bad information." I heard the school secretary often say. As well as the woman who now did payroll.

When the DOE issued an ironclad deadline to a school on some information that we, as a school, needed to have inputted into one of their brand new systems, we were in for the worst. One morning (I routinely arrived to work before 6:00 am), I received a phone call from my principal regarding something that absolutely needed to get done by that evening's "deadline" or we all faced impending doom. I was to drop everything and help the payroll secretary. When the payroll secretary arrived, she told me she was about to have a nervous breakdown because the principal had started texting her at 5:00 am and hadn't stopped since.

So we worked together. At least we tried. We had to enter specific information onto one of the DOE's new systems in order to meet a budgetary deadline that supposedly could cost our school hundreds of thousands of dollars. The system wouldn't accept the information or when it did, it wouldn't save it. Or when it said it had saved it, we'd go back later and it would ask us to begin all over again. We stayed past six o'clock that night -- a twelve hour plus day for me -- but all the phone calls, the updates, the technical tweaking, did nothing to solve the problem. And no one, and I mean not a single person anywhere knew any more than we did. All everyone told us was, "Do your best. The deadline stands."

At seven o'clock that evening, two hours past the deadline, an email went out stating that their were technological problems with the system and the deadline would be extended to a date and time that would later be announced. By the next morning, the deadline had been extended by a full week.

Had this happened one time it might have been funny in retrospect. Instead, this became the new normal. When I attempted to make clear to my boss that he should relax because his latest emergency was just another one of those impossible deadlines that would be extended hours after it passed, he would not relent as his superiors remained insistent that deadline after deadline be met -- even though it was obvious to anyone working with their systems that these systems simply weren't functioning properly.

In times like these, we always called the NYCDOE Help Desk. The call was necessary. As a school, we needed to document we had tried everything imaginable in case the deadline wasn't extended. On one of those calls, I discovered that the tech support guy I was now speaking to was in Missouri, had never been near a NYC school, and had no idea how our systems operated. His job was to refer my call to some other organization back in NYC. The guy in Missouri wasn't supposed to tell me he was in Missouri or he'd get in trouble for doing it. One operator once told me that they all had been reprimanded for revealing the fact that these operators were spread out across the Midwest.

It seemed that the NYCDOE had a penchant for putting in new systems just before a deadline. Once, they upgraded and transformed the entire grade entry system, STARS, in June just before the grades were due. We're talking over a million grades had to be entered in a two week period of time after the upgrade. Of course, there were unforeseen compatibility issues, and even the former head of STARS, now acting as a consultant, said, "They just don't think. How are you going to introduce a new system just before the grades are due and not anticipate major problems?"

If the major data systems were flawed or in some cases, as with ATS, an acronym for Automate the Schools, antiquated, how could you trust the statistics that they eventually came up with? ATS ran on what looked like a DOS interphase, and its primary structure had been introduced in 1988. The screens in ATS were solid black with green lettering. You were restricted to certain keys on the computer to input commands. Most intuitive approaches failed; you had to be shown how to use it. Even their help menus belonged in another decade.

To make matters just a little more complicated, the DOE had two major data systems for student data, which were supposed to "talk" with each other: STARS and ATS. STARS contained all the course and exam grades; ATS contained all the biographical data. The exception was summer school where all the information for classes began on ATS and then moved into STARS -- except for the state exam information, which began on ATS, ended on ATS, eventually showing up on STARS. STARS was written in SQL, a contemporary database language, and looked largely like sophisticated excel tables and was relatively user friendly. These two systems exchanged data: ATS sent over its bio data to STARS and STARS sent over the grading data to ATS -- only these systems weren't really compatible with each other.

This affected how we did business as a school. Each year, we were accountable for entering our data in these systems and receiving data back from these systems -- only the most important data came in the form of reports whose information had largely been gathered from ATS. Whether or not our school would remain open at times depended on the accuracy of the information we received and how effectively we were able to act on that information.

I never once received a data report from the city or the state regarding the students in my cohort that wasn't initially flawed, which didn't contain students who had never gone to my school or didn't contain wrong and missing information about students who had, at one time or another, attended my school. Eventually, they'd get the reports right but never until the deadline they gave you passed, when you were supposed to verify the data on that report. What this meant was you only got to see your actual data after it was too late for you to do anything about it. You couldn't dispute a single point of data, a name -- anything for that matter -- once the report had been finalized, and the finalized version of your reports always contained data, names and information, that hadn't been on any of the earlier reports.

If you projected how well your school would do based on the data in the initial reports, you were always wrong as the final report seemed to contain just enough students with bad data -- students who magically appeared after the deadline -- to foul up your school's numbers. This was a complaint I repeatedly heard at local, borough, and city wide meetings from all the data people: "Why send us reports with bad data, ask us to verify the data but then run a completely different report for our school after the deadline when it's too late for us to do anything about it?"

"That's why we ask you to verify the data."

"No. Clearly, you are able to find the flaws with the initial reports yourself and then run a different report but only when we can't do anything about our numbers. And the final report always contains more failing students. Why is that?"

"I don't know that to be the case."

"Well now you do."

Only nothing changed.

Then there were the emergencies, and we seemed for a period of several years to almost always have one going on, one that required the entire school run around meeting deadline after deadline, until exhaustion and confusion set in. We had a visitor from the state coming who was going to look over individual teacher's records; we had representatives from the city coming who were going to observe how the Special Ed students were being educated, and there were some in all of your classes; people from the Mayor's office were coming, someone from the District, from the Superintendency, from Office of Assessment -- and they might come in and talk to you.

The principal would lay out exactly what each of us were going to say and do, emphasizing this one critical point: "If we don't get this right, we're going to have a lot more people on our backs." At one point the principal began meetings with this phrase: "I don't want to alarm any of you, but it looks like they could shut us down." After five years of constant emergencies, most of us were pretty burnt out.

We once spent several weeks implementing "blended learning" models into our classrooms. The model we chose was to have students working off a group lesson, then breaking down into smaller groups or working individually, and at some point, they'd engage in an online component of the lesson, which they could continue on their own at home or outside of the classroom later during their free time. Sometimes, this involved threaded conversations online about each other's work. Throughout the process, the teacher would join the students, sometimes observing, other times critiquing, still other times modelling. Granted, it's a creative way to approach teaching, but not everyone is suited to teach that way, and not every lesson can be crafted to effectively include "blended learning." Regardless, when the visitors arrived, we would be teaching in a blended learning environment -- or whatever the flavor of the month was.

The problem with these visits was this: if you were reviewing for a test or the Regents, you may not have been in "blended learning mode." You would either have to revamp your lesson or jump to another part of your curriculum to satisfy the visitors at the expense of the continuity of what you had been doing. If you didn't model some near perfect lesson -- instead you taught what you had intended on teaching -- you ran the risk of potentially flopping during an observation because some lessons are learning experiences for the educator, especially when they unexpectedly don't succeed.

We were continuously responding to the pressures of new and ever changing standards and methods of measurement. We were assessed by observers who recorded what they saw, and their observations were presumably used to further reorganize and rethink how education should proceed. The problem was that what many observers saw, especially in schools that knew how to play the game, wasn't always real.

To further complicate issues, new metrics and standards, which seemed to have resulted in test scores going up and graduation rates increasing, were fueling many changes both in and out of the classroom -- only these results were suspect at best.

The strongest argument I can make for the 75% graduation rate in NYC from high school as being complete bullshit is the fact that we still have a 100% graduation rate from JHS. How could that be possible? Think about it. Do 25% of all students suddenly become unable to continue? Or have we not prepared them properly in the lower grades and then passed them on despite all the new regulations and reforms? Which makes more sense to you?

Many students simply don't actually read any better than before. We let kids who can barely read and write graduate, and I honestly don't believe we had any better option considering what we were up against. That sounds horrible and irresponsible.

Consider this: The co-founder of the largest privatized data company that NYC schools used to crunch their numbers was once an employee at Tweed (The brain center of the NYCDOE) where he developed his data systems. Back then he personally recommended to me, as he does to any school that can afford his services now, that your entire school should target specific students in your cohorts (the groups of students that are measured each year for graduation and test taking data) to assure that those students succeed. At least on paper. The rest doesn't matter.

In other words, if Johnny is in your graduation cohort for that year, make sure you graduate Johnny that year. Be smart and target him for success the year before, tip off all the teachers who have him and make sure they understand he needs to pass their classes, pass their portfolio based assessments, which the school completely controls, and pass the English Regents.

The only sticking point was the English Regents. As my former principal put it to me, "If we control the PBAs (portfolio based assessments), then there's no reason we shouldn't have a 100% pass rate," which we did. It was the English Regents that presented a problem. How do you get students to pass a statewide exam when some of them can barely read and write? The answer was to target the cohort students with after school sessions under threat of death and to teach them formulaic writing techniques and specific test taking skills designed to beat the exam. And that's what we did, and it worked. Students learned to beat the exam. Teachers became lenient with grading practices regarding these students, and administration created and enacted interventions to assure that this specific population would succeed.

The result was that a significant number of students continued to graduate without developing adequate literacy and numeracy skills. And colleges continued to beg us not to send them any more students who couldn't read or write.

One way the City attempted to address these issues was by creating a charter school system wherein schools could act independent of City and Union regulations while trying to innovate education. In some sense, that's what charter schools really are: an attempt to more effectively educate students by circumventing both the Union and local municipalities. It's ironic that a City should have to create a pocket of schools not strictly beholden to its own rules so that those schools might actually succeed. Unfortunately, a well known practice of charter schools was to either not accept students who they believed weren't going to succeed or to get rid of those they became convinced they couldn't work with. [1]

With the advent of the Charter school coupled with the shutting down of larger, ineffective high schools, we found our student population had begun to change. Instead of having a relatively mixed bag of students who struggled with literacy and numeracy, and other kinds of behavioral and developmental issues, we discovered that while we still had these students, a much larger portion of our incoming population now had serious literacy and numeracy issues. This shift happened almost overnight, and we weren't fully prepared for the change. After three years of these types of students flooding into our building, with all the teachers openly asking what was happening to the quality of our students, we were able to pin it on two trends: the charter schools were taking in our better students; a significant number of larger schools were closing down, being replaced by smaller and newer schools who managed to scoop up what would have been the academic upper two thirds of our student population, leaving us with the bottom of the barrel so to speak. We now found ourselves with the students that really no one else wanted or felt they could succeed with.

When the City closed down a large school, they got to circumvent the union again because they could, in effect, fire all the teachers that they couldn't fire as ineffective under the Union contract. So there's value to having a school fail. You can open up a new City school where, at one point at least, only 50% of the staff of the former school could be rehired -- although you don't really have to rehire anyone -- a ton of startup money is awarded, and a completely new administration is installed. When you open up a Charter school, you can hire and fire anyone you want *as you please* because there is no union.

Many of these Charter schools recruited teachers for 10-12 hour workdays, and these poor souls burned out within five years. Between 30 and 40 percent of these schools were closed or reorganized within the same five years it took to kill the teachers and the administrators who had attempted to get these places up and running.

For the first two years, new schools aren't responsible for their data. Instead, this data, meaning their students' pass rates, attendance rates, test scores, graduation rates, etc… is simply recorded in order to form a baseline that can be used to later measure that school's success. It's at the end of the third year that the data counts toward grading the school. By this point in time, you kind of know whether or not the school is going to succeed, but it generally takes another two years before the less successful schools close down.

As the person in my school responsible for translating transcripts, I would occasionally have to track down a student's records from one of these schools that didn't succeed. If it were a charter school that had failed and the student didn't have a transcript in hand, it could be possible that there were no records. That's right. Charter schools weren't responsible for posting their student data on the NYDOE's database. This meant that all record of a student's work could have simply vanished, and sometimes this was the case.

Don't be surprised. A colleague of mine, now long retired, once took home boxes of student files, stopping at a school event on the way home. His car was stolen. We still get calls to this day from students who claim to have graduated from our school -- only we have either an empty folder with their name on it, a partially completed record or no records at all. And we kept records.

According to the woman who organized our records room, incomplete or missing records were common. Former students just being released from prison or students who had graduated decades ago often called us for verification of their graduation, and our records could not substantiate their claims, either because they were incomplete or entirely missing.

Paper records go missing. And up until 2005, student records were primarily on paper. To further complicate matters, when the high school programs lost their state funding back in the early 2000's, these programs were given a choice: either become a diploma granting institution or forever shut your doors. Our school -- at least our central building -- received all the records from one of these programs. Supposedly. We were never able to locate most of these records. These were the records for hundreds of students, and this was just one program of dozens.

Back to the Charter schools who don't have to keep their records on the NYCDOE database: From a purely data perspective, this is suspect at best. If the success of my school is measured by a set of data points that only I can verify, well, need I say more. When you have to enter data on a universal system, you can still fudge the numbers, but there is a permanent record of what you claimed, which builds on itself year after year. When you're able to submit your data willy-nilly, while some record may exist in the form of the documents you submit, independent verification becomes more difficult. The DOE will come after you about data records entered into their database, which appear suspect, and they will ask that you independently verify your data or sometimes they will simply dispute your claims, but if none of your records are added to the DOE's database until well after the fact, that opens the door to a whole lot of "data fudging" as my mentor used to call it.

As a school, we spent decades avoiding data accountability. In the early days, our school never entered failing grades on the DOE's student database. That's correct. We entered the term "NC" which stood for "no credit." Back then, the DOE wasn't smart enough to figure out what we were doing, so it appeared as if none of our students failed any of their classes. Instead, they simply failed to complete coursework, which they later could complete, and if they needed that credit to graduate, they would and could complete it at the eleventh hour and have the credit added to their transcript. This often happened weeks before students were supposed to graduate, as some miraculously recovered huge amounts of credits at this key juncture.

The DOE caught on. Sort of. They then began to calculate credits students earned. So the grade of "NC" could no longer hide the fact that our students were failing nearly half of their classes. However, because we granted credits at a much faster rate than other schools, we were able to disguise this data point also.

We allowed our students to earn credits more easily and quickly than other schools. At one point, our students could earn 18 academic credits in a regular school year instead of the usual 12 awarded by standard high schools. With independent studies and online courses, it was conceivable that students earn as many as 22 credits in a single school year -- half the required amount to graduate in four years.

Because our students failed so many courses, we were able to conceal this. Students on an average earned over 10 credits a year, which allowed us to drop into the upper end of the transfer school bucket in terms of credits earned -- even though our actual pass rate fell in around 65%. Our low passing rate helped us escape detection from the DOE who would investigate any single student who earned more than 18 credits during a single school year. While we did have a few students accomplish this, we often added the grades at a later date, thereby further evading the DOE's scrutiny. And once we found out that 18 credits was the cutoff, we made sure no one went on record having done that unless our paper work was impeccable.

We were the number one transfer school in New York City for two years in a row -- until they threw out this rating system. Our evolution looked like this: C, then F, then A, then A with a number one ranking for two years. That covered the last five years I worked there. We had learned to play the numbers game.

"You need to look at your data carefully. Then you target those students that will make the greatest difference to your school's rating. It's a number's game," were the off-the-record words of the data guy down at Tweed.

It's not about teaching; it's not about the students: it's about the survival of your institution. After that, you can worry about doing the right thing. As a teacher, you were always at the mercy of your administration who said that they were at the mercy of the City and State.

We managed to grab onto as much money as we could as a school. One of the tricks is to selectively sign up for new initiatives -- especially the ones that appear to lack clear accountability perhaps because of their own disorganization. Programs or initiatives which grant your school plenty of flexibility while providing monies and/ or equipment are ideal. Once they start looking at you closely, you move on to the next initiative, hopefully before they can learn that you've just been taking their money. Also, the folks responsible for these initiatives have a vested interest in appearing successful, so it's in their interest to lose your school as part of the initiative, rather than have it come out that you've been bilking them for their funding while actually demonstrating no improvement at all.

Our principal -- as any successful principal does -- found ways to get money out of both City and State. On top of that, we grabbed Federal monies whenever we could, grants of any kind. And whenever possible, we grabbed private monies. At one point, we actually had more computers than we had students, but we still managed to win a computer lab from NewEgg, courtesy of an essay written by the fiance of one of our staff members about her dedication as a teacher. We were careful to keep the NewEgg people out of any of the classrooms that were overflowing with computers when they came down to our school for their PR event.

There are ways to avoid accountability on all levels. And that's what the principal's goal always was: Look good on paper then sell whatever is going on in the building to anyone who visits by pitching the success of our school as the context for what they witness. "We don't want people coming in here looking at what we're doing. Let them look at the results. As long as we're succeeding on paper, when visitors do come in, I can spin anything they see. If we don't make our numbers, then they're going to start looking at us more closely, and none of us wants that." No truer words were ever spoken by a principal.

So we hid things. When we split up into four separate schools, our sites in the Bronx, Queens and Lower Manhattan all becoming high schools in their own right, we claimed that all the missing inventory had actually disappeared from the other three sites. They did the same. Our Bronx site used to bleed equipment out of it's doors in an unprecedented manner. Laptops went missing regularly, and we once had a server walk.

There was so much missing equipment that when inventory came around, which was another job I had been asked to do, I found myself physically sick. Whenever a laptop was stolen, we were supposed to report it officially. This meant calling the police. Usually, teachers knew that equipment had gone missing but waited days, if not weeks, to report it. By then, whomever had been doing the stealing often was able to take two or three more laptops. Calling the police was an embarrassment because nobody ever knew anything. And as for the tracking program placed on the computers so that they could be recovered in the event equipment was stolen -- a program that added $100 into the price of each laptop -- this was said to me by their representative: "Yeah, good luck with that." No equipment we ever had stolen was recovered. Lack of accountability was systemic.

Bloomberg wanted to introduce strict accountability, only people aren't really prepared to learn how poorly both our schools and our students are doing. And his methods were questionable as they just forced us to become more creative about how we concealed what our school was actually doing.

Under Bloomberg, tracking students through data meant tracking teachers the same way. We had been warned that this was coming. If Johnny passed your class but didn't pass my class, the question would inevitably be asked, "What's wrong with my class?" And then, "What's wrong with me as a teacher?" If my pass rate was significantly lower than the pass rates of other teachers in the school, the question would be asked, "Why am I grading the students so hard?" I know that we asked these questions because I calculated the pass rates for teachers and departments. And when I reported my findings to the administrators, they then targeted teachers who failed too many students. While an administrator can't tell you to pass a kid, he can make it clear that you should. And if you don't, he can begin to "evaluate" you a little differently than he evaluates others but not in a way that could be proven to be biased.

We had visitors regularly, though many more when we had an "F" rating. City and State evaluators would come into your classrooms and departmental meetings and ask you to use the latest jargon to describe what you were trying to do in your classroom with your students. You can't say, "I'm trying to teach them to read." You have to say, "I'm teaching critical thinking skills and literary analysis using literary elements." You can't say, "I'm trying to build a foundation on which the students can tackle more sophisticated reading and writing assignments." You have to say, "I'm scaffolding." And you can't say, "I'm teaching them to write essays." You have to say, "I'm teaching them to build an argument through the use of supporting evidence."

As a teacher, you adapt. If they tell you to "scaffold" and "differentiate" then you keep on teaching the way you've been teaching, only now you become more conscious of how to answer the loaded questions you're asked by evaluators who are often the same burnt out administrators that failed at running their own schools.

The Bloomberg business model implies that education can be run like a business, and the measurement of a school's success is efficiency. Once you introduce the concept of efficiency on a business level into any school, you have to measure outcomes. Test scores, attendance, passing rates or credit accumulation and graduation rates become the indicators of those outcomes – not whether anyone has actually learned anything. So schools, in order to survive, often push students on, which is the very problem that these types of reorganization were designed to prevent.

We learned early into this new evaluation system, if a NYC school didn't make certain state indicators, the state threatened to close it down, but if that same school didn't make a different set of city indicators, the city would close it down even more quickly. There was actually a point in time when a school could have been doing well under state standards but ended up being shut down for failure to meet city standards – though more often the reverse ended up being true. If your school received an "A" on its city report card, which had been the case with our school on one occasion, but had failed to comply to the state mandate, you were in trouble. The last thing you wanted to mention to the state, who was threatening to close you down, was that the city gave you an "A" on your last report card. It played out like a challenge, and the state people basically let you know that "A" or no "A," they were coming after you. The state didn't care what the city thought and visa versa.

There were advantages to being on the state's shit list of schools. Being on SINI, (Schools In Need of Improvement) garnished you additional funding. And for a while, the way things worked for alternative schools went something like this:

Your success as a school according to the State of New York depended on your graduation rate, your pass rate on state exams and your student participation rate in those same exams. If you failed to meet any one of those indicators two years in a row, your school ended up on level one of SINI. To get off level one, you had to meet that same indicator two years in a row.

Once you hit level one of the ladder to limbo, your school found itself entitled to more funding from the state. This was a good thing. Level two of SINI brought even more funding, as did level three. On some level, it's Freakonomics: Create a solution for a problem that generates additional funding for those schools in need of that solution (in effect, you've introduced financial incentives into an equation) and you unwittingly perpetuate the problem in a new and sometimes unrecognizable way.

What incentive would a school have to do better if it meant that by "improving" they would lose funding? So if the school, a year after ending up on SINI, managed to make its key indicators, they found themselves "frozen" on SINI, funding still intact. If during the year that followed that one, they failed to meet that indicator, they *still* remained frozen on SINI. So it was possible, as was the case with my school, to remain on level three of SINI frozen, forever teetering on the brink of shutdown, with additional funding flowing in as if through a broken pipe while the school simply stood still in the eyes of the state.

The alternative schools posed a real problem for both the city and the state. Graduation rates had been traditionally measured by a school's ability to graduate a student within four years. That meant a death sentence for alternative schools who often took "failing" students from other schools after they had been there three or more years. The sending school wanted them off their state list as holding onto them meant bad data for that school; however, once we accepted that student, we often had a year or less to graduate the student or that student translated into bad data for us.

In short, if a student transferred out of your school before BEDS day (a day in October: the first Thursday or the very last day of the month, depending on whether it was the city or state's BEDS day) of his fourth year of high school and was accepted into another school, then the receiving school became accountable for that student's performance. This simply didn't seem fair. How could any school manage to graduate a "failing" student in one year when another school had "failed" at moving the same student past the tenth grade in three years?

On some level, you would think accepting these students would be a disincentive for alternative schools – later to become known as transfer schools – but it wasn't for many of us. We simply ignored what the state said, played the SINI game and tried to work as best as we could with the students no one else wanted.

Early on, the state found itself in a quandary. If they held alternative schools to the same standards as traditional high schools, they would eventually end up closing many of them down. Then where would these "failing" students go? And what would that do to the state's graduation rate if more than 35% of its students simply never graduated high school? Wouldn't that be an indictment against the state's educational system?

When I entered my last school in 2007, the state had long ago recognized the inequity of measuring an alternative school by the same criteria as a regular school. Alternative schools were measured by a different set of indicators. As a principal, you were given two indicators and had to select a third one from a list. The first indicator was graduation rate; the second indicator was the pass rate on state exams and the third indicator, which our principal got to choose, was suspension rate. As our school had four sites in three boroughs (Queens, Bronx and two in Manhattan), whenever a student did anything worthy of a suspension, we had that student transferred to a different site. Only the very serious cases warranted superintendent suspensions, and we had almost none of those. We eliminated those kinds of students through our meticulous intake process.

Back then, there were little tricks to meeting the other two indicators. If you failed to meet a specific indicator, such as the graduation rate, which the state had set for you, then the next year you could satisfy this indicator by simply improving your prior year's performance by 10%.

Students were divided into cohorts. These cohorts were determined by their ninth grade entry date. If your current year's cohort managed a 10% graduation rate, when the state had required you graduate 75% of your students, then that next year, you only had to graduate 10% more than what you had previously managed, which meant your target graduation rate would be 11%. This was called "safe harbor". Now let's look at the numbers. Say your school had 1200 students on register. Generally around 300 would be in any one cohort, which meant if you have graduated only 10% of that 300, which is 30 students, failing to meet the state requirement, you only had to graduate 33 of the next 300 the following year in order to make "safe harbor". So you identified and targeted those students. In an alternative school, with the population you were dealing with, it often proved difficult to make those numbers two years in a row. The result: your school remained "frozen" on SINI, receiving tons of state monies, while teetering on the edge of shutdown, yet always managing to fall backwards away from the precipice during the critical years.

The same proved true with the pass rate on the English Regents. Target key students in that cohort and make sure that whatever happened, you didn't overshoot your mark. That's right, you never wanted too many students to graduate from any one cohort or have an excessive number of students pass the English Regents as it could prove problematic when trying to meet the numbers in the succeeding years. (We were a portfolio school, so all other subject areas had their regents requirements satisfied by students completing and presenting portfolios. That meant we were able to control all other subject areas. Even if the kid was nearly retarded, he could, with help, put together and present a portfolio.)

In reality, the school often hovered at around a 13% to 15% graduation rate, losing 1/3 of the students who came in within the first year. So this meant that we never really had to improve. At a 14% true graduation rate, we only had to hit 15% the following year. However, the next year, we'd have to hit 17%, and we could never meet that number. So on the year we missed, it worked particularly well to keep our graduation rate down around 10%. First of all, since we couldn't make the targeted rate anyway, no harm real was done. We remained frozen on SINI, so we didn't fall further down the ladder of doom, still kept our funding, and we only had to think about the upcoming year. The next year we had to outperform the prior year by 10%, which translated into graduating around eight students from the cohort from each of our four sites. We could make those numbers. So around and around we went, frozen, then almost not frozen on SINI -- state funding abundant and intact.

How many students we had in the school also determined how much funding we received. This allowed another scam to be perpetrated by crafty administrators. In the 1980's, you simply had to have a specific number of student on register as of the first Thursday in October or the on the last day in October, depending whether or not you were considering the city or state cut off dates. Once that date passed, students could literally disappear and there would be no financial consequences. So schools like the ones I worked for – the alternative schools – always loaded up their registers before the October cutoffs, and then they sat back while the school emptied out. A program of 250 students could literally have fewer than 150 students in the building by the time February or March rolled around. And often the numbers would drop even lower by May or June. Still, we received funding as if all 250 students were being serviced.

In reality, our population couldn't function in a full building. They needed smaller classes with a relaxed atmosphere. So no one really did much back then about the attendance. I once taught an afternoon class than never had more than 12 students in it. I had probably never seen 10 of the students on register ever. In that atmosphere, I proved successful at getting students to work, to pass state exams, and to graduate. Had everyone shown up, the class would have probably been unmanageable because of the nature of the students and their specific learning and emotional needs. We were successful on paper because we capitalized on the opportunities produced by our failures, and we shamelessly worked the system. Eventually, the city and state cracked down on this, and your school had to maintain its numbers.

One of cleverest things I was able to perpetrate for my principal was concealing the fact that we had continued to offer interdisciplinary courses after the city had cracked down on schools for the liberality with which they had been awarding credits. With interdisciplinary courses, a student could take a single class whose credit could be applied toward meeting graduation requirements in as many as five different subject areas. At one point, the DOE even had a system that allowed you to do this. When the nature of how interdisciplinary credits were awarded was investigated, it was found that most schools were not awarding credits properly, so the new rules required that we only award credits in a maximum of two different areas. And you had to use the DOE's system to do this, which would result in a periodic checkup from their auditors. Before the crackdown, students could earn health, art, music, social studies or English credits for their advisory, which was basically an extended homeroom where you and your students often did a kind of talk therapy and occasionally class projects, which would be presented to the class and sometimes to the entire school. The interdisciplinary crackdown ended this blatant awarding of credits across the board for a single course.

In true interdisciplinary course offerings, the teacher gets to decide how credits are awarded based on the work that the student has done. In our school, advisors got to pick and choose where credits were placed, which a student received from an interdisciplinary course, based *on the individual student's graduation needs.* That was completely illegal, but we managed to conceal this by having a separate data storage system online coupled with an inhouse database which I created to translate those courses into the credits students needed. At the end of each semester, I uploaded the final list of completed credits to the DOE's database from my database after all the credits had been distributed behind the scenes. When the DOE cracked down, I created an even more elaborate data system that completely concealed the fact we were still offering interdisciplinary courses -- with the help of a principal from the Bronx and a guy down at the DOE's data systems. As a school, we hid from the NYCDOE that we were working around them every single year after that. This system of awarding credits where a student needed them had historically helped us to graduate students who could barely be persuaded to show up, so continuing to use it despite the DOE's edicts was critical to our success on paper.

An unfortunate consequence of our educational practices was that colleges began to beg us, specifically asking the administrators of one of our sites, to please not send them any more students who were illiterate. Yes, we were graduating some students who could barely read and write and had been all along.

---

[1] *Why Charter Schools Have High Teacher Turnover*, City Limits, 8-20-2014

Chapter Twelve

Investigations
Set a thief to catch a thief...

"There's an investigation going on right now, and you're going to be called as a witness."

"A witness?"

"Yes. A witness. You're not under investigation. I am. I could be fired for having this conversation with you."

"Go on."

"We're not having this conversation."

"What conversation?"

"Exactly. I want to tip you off about what they're going to ask you. They want to know about data entry, specifically about the PBA grades and how we entered them. They can't, I repeat, they can't, find out how we entered those grades, especially around the time our schools split up."

"So what am I supposed to do if they ask me about the PBA grades?"

"Answer their questions."

"Answer their questions?"

"Yes. But don't volunteer information. If you get an opening, explain to them how STARS works. What you have to do to enter grades in STARS. The way you always try to explain it to me. By the end of it, he won't know his own name."

I'm sitting with my union rep outside the Office of Special Investigations.

"They're not after you. They're after your principal. Just give them what they want and they'll leave you alone."

Inside the office, the questions piled up.

"Do you do grade entry?"

"Yes."

"Do you ever change grades?"

"Yes."

"Why?"

"If a teacher or administrator comes to me and shows me evidence that a grade was either mistakenly entered or that a student did work which warrants a grade change, then I change the grade."

"Has the principal ever asked you to change grades?"

"Rarely and then never without documented evidence. It's mostly the teachers who come to me."

"But you have changed grades based on what the principal has asked you?"

"Yes."

"How do you enter grades?"

"Through the grade entry screen in STARS."

"And there's a record of every grade you enter?"

"Yes."

"Do you enter PBA grades?"

"Through the grade entry screen?"

"Yes."

"No." I entered them as transcript updates through a separate screen.

"You never enter PBA grades?"

"Not through the grade entry screen in STARS, no."

His next question should have been, "Do you enter PBA grades any other way?" and that would have been my principal's job. Instead, I explained to him how STARS worked.

"You see, at the end of the semester, I enter all the grades for all the students. It's complicated because we have interdisciplinary courses and one class might count for as many as five different subject areas."

"Five subject areas."

"Yes. One class could count for civics or art or music or health or English."

"One class."

"So each grade has to be broken down into what subject area that passing grade is going to be applied to."

"In STARS. Using the grade entry screen."

"Using the interdisciplinary table."

"The interdisciplinary table."

"Yes. This table shows what each class could count for."

"The interdisciplinary table. Not the grade entry screen. You don't enter grades through the grade entry screen?"

"I do enter grades through the grade entry screen but not without first using the interdisciplinary table to expand the classes."

"Expand the classes."

The union rep jumped in to help. "Each class counts for five classes."

"Five classes."

"Potentially." I added.

"So a student is actually in five classes at once?" the investigator asked.

"If he's taking five different classes, he could be in up to 25 different virtual classes."

"Virtual classes."

"Those are online classes," the rep offered.

"Not exactly. They are classes that only exist on the STARS server. The student only sits in five actual classes."

"But he gets credit for 25 classes?" the investigator wanted to know.

"He could get credit for any of 25 classes, but he usually only gets credit for seven or eight?"

"What happens to the rest of the classes?"

"Nothing. They aren't really there."

"They aren't?"

"They're only on the STARS server."

"But not online." the Union rep offered.

The investigator had begun to sweat. He picked up his coffee and his hand was shaking.

"Any more questions."

"So you don't enter the PBA grades?"

"The PBA grades."

"Yes. Through the… grade entry screen?"

"No I don't."

"That's all I have for you then."

Chapter Thirteen

Personal Demons
You cannot escape yourself

In my fourth year of teaching, I was offered a literacy class, and I accepted. For five years, I developed a literacy curriculum, sometimes working with my grad professor at City College, other times with my supervisor at the school who gave me all the support and freedom to create as I might need.

Most of my literacy students were from other countries, though only a few had been English as a Second Language students. All of my students spoke some form of English, often learned in their country of origin. I had a Guyanese girl who read on a third grade level even though she was 19, and I had a young man, originally ESL, who read on a second grade level -- the lowest level the assessment we administered could detect. And there was Foxy, a 20 year old who had been born here; English was her first language, but she simply couldn't read or write beyond a third grade level.

"I feel dumb. It's embarrassing." She once said to me.

"You're not dumb. Literacy is a skill, like riding a bike. If you didn't know how to ride a bike, would you call yourself dumb?"

"No."

"So learn the skill."

"By reading little kiddy books? My sister is in JHS school, and she makes fun of the books I'm reading."

"How'd you learn to ride a bike? With training wheels? Eventually, they came off. You won't be reading kiddy books for much longer, but you have to begin somewhere."

She still didn't seem convinced. "Look, there's no direct connection between literacy and intelligence. You can read well and still be an idiot."

"Joe, I'm 20 years old and my little sister is reading books I can't."

"Let's figure out how you learn. Right now, write in your journal about how you're struggling. Write down exactly the kinds of things we spoke about right here."

"Okay. But what do you mean, 'figure out how I learn?'"

"Someone missed something along the way with you. Until we can either figure out how you learn or simply teach you all over again, you're going to continue to struggle. Personally, I'd like to help you figure out how you learn."

"Why?"

"Because then you'll be able to use what you find out in this class in all your other classes and outside of the classroom as well. Think of it this way: You look at the world differently than other people. The different way you see the world, that you learn about things, that's the key."

"I like that."

In those days, I made my students write journals everyday, and I offered them the opportunity to share what they'd written. I had them in one room for two hours straight, and I needed to have a structure in place that allowed them time to read, write, and reflect. Journals were read in class and students shared about each other's lives -- even if the journals were personal.

Foxy was a "street" person, involved in or hanging around all kinds of criminal activities, but mostly she wrote about life at home with her mother who drank or with her sister, who she admired for being smart, and occasionally one of her uncles who liked hanging out, getting high and making promises to women he would never keep.

"My uncle's a player." she once wrote. Everyone laughed. After that, she liked sharing her journals.

I enjoyed watching Foxy write in her journal as she often put down the pen, shook her hand and then picked it up with the other hand and simply continued to write. There was no difference in her handwriting whether she used her left or right hands. When I asked her about it, she acted surprised.

"I've always been this way."

"You don't feel more comfortable with one hand or the other?"

"Nope."

One day, I got an idea. "I want all of you to write about something you love to do -- something that you're good at. You can even show us if you want. You know, bring in an example of your work or show us some pictures."

"I'm not good at anything."

"Don't you like to do anything?"

"I like to sleep."

"Everybody has something they enjoy doing, that they've been doing for a while. Think about it: what makes you feel good when you do it?"

"Getting high."

"Besides getting high."

"Sex."

"Great. Don't write about sex."

"Yeah, but I'm good at it."

"That's a lot of information."

"What do you like to do?"

"I like hiking through the mountains. When I walk through the woods, something happens to me. I see things other people don't see."

"You see bigfoot?" One student wanted to know.

"I can pause in one place, just get quiet, and then I notice animals all around me."

"That's not really working for us, Joe."

"Okay. I like to cook."

"Me too."

"I thought you weren't good at anything."

"I didn't say I was good at it. I said I liked to do it."

"So write about that. I want you to tell me about the first time you ever became interested in cooking. Describe that first experience. That's your first paragraph. In the next paragraph, tell me about what happened as you began to cook more. How did you go about getting better at it? In the third paragraph…"

"Jesus, Joe, how long you want this frigging thing to be?"

"Yeah, man, you're OD'ing."

"We'll take our time on it. I'll help you every step of the way. And you'll help each other."

"You gonna write it for me?"

"I'm not gonna help you that much."

"The only way you're getting three paragraphs out of me is if you write them yourself."

"In the third paragraph, I want you to tell me what cooking means to you now. Tell me how often you cook, how it feels when you're cooking, who you cook for -- anything you want to add that you think is important."

"We all writing about cooking?"

"No. Each of you is writing about one thing you're either really good at or that you enjoy doing."

Back then, I had been taught this learning model: I do, you watch; I do, you help. You do, I help; you do, I watch. So I would write a paragraph on the board for them. Next, we would write one together. I would elicit the sentences from students around the room, sometimes changing some of the language but keeping the ideas intact. In their own work, I would help them individually, making corrections to language and suggestions, but I began to work with keeping their voices intact, even if it meant leaving in some of the questionable language and grammar. There was no value to changing everything at once as if left students who already felt they couldn't write believing that all the more and becoming discouraged. Eventually, they wrote on their own. And as they wrote more, I noticed that their language and facility with translating their thoughts to the page simply improved on its own. The glaring and recurring problems with language, structure, and grammar that remained I addressed in group lessons, often using student work on handouts. So students ended up correcting their own and each other's work as part of a lesson. I found that after the initial shock, they enjoyed seeing their sentences or paragraphs or even entire essays on a worksheet that we as a class used to learn.

The first major writing project for the literacy class took a full week, most of it accomplished in class with lots of help and encouragement. To break things up, I added mini lessons, using some of their work to teach basic grammar and structure. In then end, they read their essays aloud. On a whim, I hung them up on the outside bulletin board. I caught them reading their own essays from time to time. While I personally never wanted to bother with bulletin boards of any sort, for these students whose work had probably never been displayed, this meant something.

One day, I had this conversation with Foxy. "Joe. I can't do this. I'm never gonna get any good at this."

"And how did you learn to cook again?"

She smiled. "I spent a lot of time working at it."

"And?"

"And I had people help me."

"And?"

"I kept at it."

"Okay. So why is this any different?"

"I don't like doing this. I like cooking."

"Exactly. But it doesn't mean you can't learn this. You have to do the same things you did to get good at cooking: Stick to it, put in the time, allow for mistakes, be patient with yourself. Acknowledge that it's hard."

"What does acknowledge mean?"

"Admit it to yourself."

"Why didn't you just say that? Why you gotta use those big words to say something simple?"

Once, on a trip to Dorney Park, nine of our students got caught "stealing" stuffed animals and the state police were called. One of my colleagues said, "Leave them here. They deserve what they get for embarrassing us."

I asked the trooper what had happened.

"They wandered into a roped off area and found some old stuffed animals."

"I'm sorry. They're a little rough around the edges but they're basically good kids." I looked over at Foxy who was one of the nine. "What can I do to settle this? Can I pay for the things they took?"

The trooper looked over at the park official who said. "Yeah, that would take care of it."

"What are we talking about here?"

The representative from Dorney Park spoke. "Four dollars and eighty five cents."

"That's it?" I looked over at Foxy and then asked the trooper. "Did they give you a hard time?"

"They did. They used foul language and were very confrontational."

"I'm sorry for that. It's just the city wearing off of them. I wish we could just wash it all away so we could find out what's underneath, but they need it back home to survive."

"I think I understand. We really don't want to get anyone in trouble."

"Thank you."

Later, Foxy said to me, "I knew you wasn't gonna leave us."

"No." She was holding one of the animals in her arms, embracing it as if it were a child. I would run into her one day on the train years after I stopped working in Bushwick, and she would be pregnant and struggling with addiction. I'd be with my wife, and Foxy would ask for a kind of help that I couldn't give.

Our school was squeezed into the back end of the second floor of a Junior High School. One section of our school space was simply a large room, which we had divided into five separate classrooms using partitions. These were short partitions -- some not even partitions at all – simply bookcases and filing cabinets lined up in a row.

Teaching in that one large room grew progressively more difficult as the morning wore on for the classes grew louder by the hour. By the end of the third period, you could easily hear the teachers on both sides of you teaching their lessons. Most teachers stood while they taught, so you could simply turn and see your colleagues. By the last period of the day, the noise level had risen to a deafening cacophony.

On Fridays, it was particularly difficult because that was when some teachers, exhausted by an entire week of this, decided to show a film to their class. If the film were being taught in one of the middle rooms, students from classes on both sides would line up, simply standing with their arms folded on the top the filing cabinets or bookcases, watching the film. If someone next to you were showing a film, you had no shot at teaching anything. You were better off watching the film.

The entire school taught from 9:00 am straight through until 12:40 without a break: five classes in a row. At 12:40, all students were dismissed, and teachers went to lunch or simply disappeared. Never once during those first few years were we required to do anything from 12:40 until 2:40, which is when we went home for the day. In theory, this free time consisted of our prep, lunch period and administrative assignment all bunched together. We were supposed to use that time to plan and prepare, which some of us did; many of us hung out, went home and came back. Once, three of us went to strip club, smoked a joint and drank before returning to the building to punch out.

The trip to the strip club involved three of us squeezing into my friend's two seater, driving from Bushwick Brooklyn into Lower Manhattan, and at 1:00 in the afternoon hanging out in a topless bar, drinks in one hand and dollar bills in the other.

These were difficult times for me personally as I really didn't even suspect that I had a problem with alcohol. I had some inkling that the cocaine was trouble, but that was about it. Hanging out with my colleagues in the middle of a work day, drinking and getting high, clouded the issue further.

While my drinking was already out of control, with episodic incidents to confirm this, I couldn't see it or didn't want to see it. One evening I go so drunk and high at my colleague's house, the guy I went to the strip club with, that I barely could make it home. I tried taking the train, but when I ran into students of mine who were returning from an evening prep class, I just got off the train to avoid them, which turned out to be a mistake. I ended up at the topless bar, spending my last dollars and then taking a cab home. When I didn't have the money to pay for the cab, I found myself in a confrontation with the two drivers. One threatened me with a baseball bat and stole all my belongings, including the film that I was supposed to show the next day in school. That was a low morning for me, but it passed into that blank area where I hid all the things I couldn't face about myself.

One of the students who I had seen the night before was in the class where I was supposed to show the film, and he asked me if I had lost it the night before after he'd seen me. I told him yes, but when other students questioned him about it, he simply said, "Joe was on his personal time." I had the reputation as a drunk already although I didn't know it.

On another occasion, the nephew of my cocaine dealer ended up as a student in my homeroom. To further complicate matters, he threw a half full gallon jug of water out the window, striking a passing woman in the leg. While I hadn't witnessed it personally, several students came to me and told me who had done it. None of them, however, would come forward formally and identity him. I found out through his uncle that he was the enforcer for a big time drug kingpin in the neighborhood, probably came to school carrying a gun, and while he would speak to his nephew for me, he warned that I should avoid crossing the kid as he was dangerous.

I went to the Center Administrator, who was livid about what had happened, and I identified the kid as the culprit.

"You have witnesses?"

"Yes."

"Well I need to speak with them."

"None of them are willing to come forward."

"Well there's nothing I can do."

"The kid is dangerous."

"How do you know this?"

"From his uncle. We play cards together. This kid is a gangster. No one will speak against him."

"Well, I'm sorry, Joe, I can't do anything about it unless someone is willing to come forward."

"Timothy, I'm trying to warn you that we have a dangerous kid on our hands. He is capable of hurting people, hurting you or me. Do you understand what I'm saying to you?"

"Did he threaten anyone?"

"No. He doesn't have to. It's implied."

"I'm sorry. That's just not good enough."

"My word isn't good enough?"

"I believe that you believe what you're saying is true. But I can't throw a kid out of school on that alone. There's nothing I can do."

"That's your final answer? You're not going to do anything?"

"I'm sorry, but unless someone comes forward, there's absolutely nothing I can do."

So I went to the kid directly.

"I know you through the water out the window."

"How do you know?"

"It doesn't matter."

"Well, I know who you are."

"I know. And that's okay."

"I want to be honest here with you. What you did wasn't okay.

It made me look bad. And you could have really done some damage to that lady."

"She's alright."

"Yeah. I went to the AP and I tried to have you thrown out of the school. He refused. I think you know that no one will speak out against you so there's nothing anyone can do."

"So what you gonna do?"

"I want to squash it. Now." He just looked at me. "But I also want to tell you this. If something like this ever happens again, I'm gonna handle it my own way."

"Fair enough." We shook hands.

An hour later, the Center Administrator threw the kid out of the school. He stood outside the building with one of his friends, calling me out, believing I had gone back on my word.

I found my Vietnam Vet buddy, Johnny, and we went down stairs together. When we exited the building, the custodian, who was also a Vietnam Vet and one of our drinking buddies, happened to be outside working with some heavy wrenches -- only I didn't really see anything specific he was working on.

By then, the gangster and his partner had left, and later that day I went to the Uncle and explained what had happened. He told me not to worry about it as the kid didn't really care that he was thrown out of school. It was one of the first times I'd ever feared for my life as a teacher.

Boundaries were lax. Teachers were very familiar with students. I had them over to my house, and my wife and I made them dinner. As did my colleagues. We wouldn't think anything of visiting a student at home. My colleagues and I went to birthday parties and christening; we attended weddings and funerals. I worked there for nine years, through my divorce. I had one student who came to my new apartment to watch the fights. His mother did my sewing for me. She regularly hemmed my pants.

One of my colleagues, John, who was in his 40's at the time, would often have his office door closed. That was the signal. You knew what to expect; yet, whenever I knocked to speak with him, he'd casually tell me to come in. I can't recall a single instance when he didn't have a former female student sitting on his lap, his arms wrapped around her. "This is my 2nd wife." He'd say, introducing me to her. Or "This is my 3rd wife." He absolutely had no shame. Another of my colleagues told me that the former Center Administrative had interviewed him for his current position with a female staff member sitting on his lap.

Our students were 17 to 22 years old. Now and then we slipped someone in who was somewhat older. Most of the teachers were in their early 20s. It truly was a different era.

One year we had the large room turned into five smaller rooms – only one room ended up being a narrow corridor that allowed one desk in sideways with just enough space to squeeze in front of it to reach the back of the room. That's where I taught my literacy class to my 12 students. They all had reading levels between 2nd and 3rd grades. No one read better than that. I had to teach these students to pass two state exams: a reading exam and a writing exam.

The deal my boss and I came to was this: I got to keep those students in that room for two hours straight, take them on as many trips as I wanted, and be as creative as I could with whatever approaches I decided to try. At the end of a year, I had a 90% pass rate on the writing exam. I had taught them how to beat the test. They still could hardly read; perhaps they had improved by two grade levels or so – just enough to be able to crack the writing exam. In exchange for my time and effort, they left me alone as a teacher. The reading exam proved harder to tackle. It actually required that students read – something many of them were unwilling to do.

Eventually, I went to work on that one too. The exam consisted of CLOZE reading passages -- passages where a single word would be left out of a sentence periodically throughout the passages, and on the side students were given a selection of five choices. The first few passages were relatively easy, but they later passages became progressively more difficult. The only strategy that I could come up with to assist students who read at a 4th grade reading level was this: you have to get the first 28 - 35 questions correct. Passing required 48 correct answers out of 70 questions.

I taught contextual clues, vocabulary, test taking skills, decoding skills: as I taught to the exam, I learned from my students what skills they lacked, and then I found other ways to teach those skills outside of the exam. I had them practice portions of the exam after each lesson, reminding them of the skill they had been taught and then modeling how to use that skill throughout the passage. Finally,

I had students tackle the questions aloud, walking them through modeling the skill for the rest of the class until everyone began to get it.

It was a slow and grueling process that often left us exhausted. Two hours is a long time to hold students in a tiny room with no space to move around in. That's why it was so important to develop relationships with them, to gain their trust, and to encourage them in things that existed outside of academics.

So we did everything together: planned international food days, where my students, who were from a multitude of Central and South American countries, as well as the Caribbean, brought in dishes I had never heard of: delicious crab legs cooked in a green sauce, mofongo, and coconut rice with gandules. It was a feast.

We went ice-skating and roller skating; we traveled to the Bronx Zoo and ate in Little Italy in the Bronx. I had them over to my home for an early dinner where they ate all the Italian foods I could make – sometimes foods they had never seen or heard of. We saw plays in the City, worked with the Manhattan Theater Club or saw Pace University productions of famous works such as Gaslight, where the entire first act we watched as the investigator's mustache kept slipping slowly off his face. I don't think anyone in the giggling audience could notice anything else, but it was wonderful.

We even planned the first of many trips to what would later become the Senior Trip for the school: Great Adventure and then Dorney Park. Each year we travelled to one or the other on Brooklyn-Queens Day, when our school, located in Brooklyn, had the day off. They were beautiful times when I defied the Principal, who warned me not to collect money for this trip, which was illegal. When you tell an alcoholic not to do something, it may become an incentive.

We collected money during lunch, after school – and during the day. The first trip five teachers conspired together. I rented a 20-person van and another colleague brought his father's van, which held as many. Three cars joined us. The second trip we rented a full sized bus. By the fifth year, the Principal showed up. He drove with us in his own car and spent the entire day at the park, watching what went on. I received a letter of commendation in my file for orchestrating such an event, which would forever be known as the "Senior Trip". Two years later, several students from another school in NYC were killed in a fire at a nearby theme park, and the DOE forbid any more such trips.

Before the senior trip ended, the drinking caught up with me again. Three days before one trip, I went on a bender. I just kept drinking and calling in sick. The morning of the trip I had almost no money left. I had spent it all -- including about half of the money for the bus. My wife at the time simply wrote me a check for the amount to cover the cost of the bus and allowed me to keep the couple hundred I still had as pocket change. I reeked of alcohol and had kept such bad records that I couldn't keep track of who had actually paid. One student seemed particularly hostile that I insisted he pay as I had no record of his ever having handed me money. He eventually coughed up the amount, so I never was sure whether he just had counted on my ineptness to allow him to squeeze onto the bus without having to pay the money or whether he had paid and I had unfairly squeezed the extra money out of him. I promised to buy him food at the park, and when he couldn't find me later on, he said the other students suggested that I was probably off someplace getting drunk.

There is a certain amount of self-hatred that lies underneath most drunks. Anyone's approval is better than your own contempt. I had been wounded, first as a child, but then as a young man and eventually as an adult. Perhaps most people are on some level. What it turned into with me is this condition where I created situations in my life that would further wound me, confirming my own helplessness -- only I didn't know that I was driven by these internal states. I was either reawakening old wounds or causing new pain. In the end, it turned out that I had been suffering from PTSD my entire life, but despite all the therapy, it had gone undiagnosed and thus untreated. The alcoholism and the addiction were maladaptive stress management systems that I used to cope with the emotional distress experienced from "an unpredictable and ambiguous world", appropriately described as such by a Jungian psychologist. I had what Shizen Young referred to as "undigested emotions". I needed to find ways to compassionately process them.

PTSD is tricky and treacherous. The aching core of my being colored my perceptions. What existed inside of me I often experienced as powerful and sometimes dangerous outside forces acting upon me. This vulnerability and this unrelenting ache of my soul I countered with unforgiving contempt: my father beating me naked down the stairs, whipping me mercilessly with the belt; the terrified child cowering helplessly under the unforgiving lash. The repugnance that I felt toward myself for having deserved to be treated in these ways, for having allowed myself to be broken, feeling deeply ashamed of what I was as a human being, emanated outward, creating a kind of radar that scanned the world, helping me to find people and build situations for myself that would leave me victimized. When I drank and snorted coke, for a while, it went away.

Addiction became the dysfunctional method I had chosen to manage my pain, my fear of intimacy, as close relations with others had historically proven dangerous; yet, being unable to meaningfully and regularly connect with other human beings and deepen that connection over time left me aching with loneliness and at times desperate: I needed your approval, and I was willing to work myself to death to get it, willing to place myself at your mercy -- only I never imagined that I had been doing this to myself. I always thought that you had been taking advantage of me -- not that I had been giving myself away.

Despite my flagrant flaws, and sometimes because of them, a trust developed between myself and my students. I was a drunk, but I would, to the best of my ability, try to help you.

Many of the other teachers, despite their shortcomings, made it clear that they would, above all other things, struggle to help their students, and it was through the creation of this kind of community between staff and students, a community that by today's standards cuts along the edge and sometimes flagrantly violates many of the Department of Education's protocols and ethical requirements, that allowed our school to become relatively successful and flourish. Teachers bonded together, despite differences, out of respect for each other's craft and love of the students, and the school -- creating a safe haven in a crumbling neighborhood -- and it truly became something to behold, even if we, as individuals, often failed in our own lives.

Chapter Fourteen

To Be or Not to Be

Eventually, our school, Bushwick Outreach, one site of a six-sited program that existed in four boroughs, began to send students to college prepared. A young social studies teacher took on the responsibility of making sure that happened. By the end of three years of his tenure in the position of college advisor, he had 90% of our students applying to college, 75% of them getting accepted, with nearly 50% of those who had been accepted going to state and private institutions via some sort of scholarship. I didn't always like the guy, and I know he didn't always like me, but I knew in my heart that he was great for the community, so I spoke highly of him.

One day after I returned from a three day drinking binge, dragging my broken self down a hallway, he stopped me and genuinely asked if I was alright. It touched me. It made me remember what he had on his wall: The first step in combating a problem is to identify that problem; then you have to understand the problem; finally, you have to accept things as they are: until these things are done, you will remain helpless to change anything.

I once sat in a rehab, where week after week, as I slowly came to, I had become conscious that the counselor gave the exact same graduation speech to every graduate. It went like this: The individual getting ready to leave rehab would stand up in the middle of the circle across from his counselor who held a coin. On that coin was the serenity prayer. The counselor would read the entire prayer and then say, without fail, the same exact thing to each client: you have to develop the wisdom to know the difference between what you can change and what you can't change.

So when I stood across from my counselor, I knew what was coming – only this is what happened: "YOU, YOU'RE PROBLEM IS ACCEPTANCE!." He yelled it at me. It brought me back to Asad's wall. "You have to accept things for what they are or you are truly fucked." The counselor actually said that to me. I still struggle with acceptance today.

When I ended up in rehab years before, the drinking pattern appeared to be different. Back then, I repeatedly got drunk with the custodians after work, telling my first wife that I was working late. Those were ugly times. I once stood across the street from my school, dead drunk and still drinking, yelling up at the building, at the Principal who had looked out the window and told me to please go home – a place he had tried to send me earlier for my own good. I wasn't written up for any of it. People joked in the meeting how I would be teaching "Days of Wine and Roses" the next semester. The following day I came in with my tail between my legs, riddled with shame. It passed, and I got drunk again.

This time, when I went off the rails and began drinking, I simply stopped going to work. I knew that if I had continued sober, I would have ended up doing something either at work or at home that I could never take back. It had been that serious. I had changed jobs to become part of a startup school, had a baby and bought a house -- all within a three month period of time. And all I could think of was escaping. The job was untenable. I'd spend an hour taking my son to my mother-in-law's, banging on her door to wake her up as she'd frequently taken too much medication the night before, more time looking for parking, and another thirty minutes on the remaining commute, only to do it in reverse coming home. My days were never ending and unpredictable, and while I was making AA meetings every single day, I couldn't sustain it.

I shared openly about not being able to continue, both at home and in AA, and here's what I was told, "You can do this."

"No I can't."

In AA: "You're doing great."

"Didn't you hear what I just shared?"

"You sound good, kid."

At home: "It may not seem like it, but you'll get through this."

It's tough when you tell the truth and people assure you that it isn't the truth.

During my first marriage, I would come to work frequently drunk from the night before or severely hungover. I told myself it was okay because I was showing up. I would often stop drinking at 5:59 am, convincing myself that I hadn't been drinking that day, so it was okay. I reeked of alcohol. Everyone knew I was a drunk. I harbored delusions that people, especially my students, didn't know.

What made it particularly complicated is how consumed by the cocaine addiction I had become. My first wife used to keep a drug allowance for me in "The Consumer Reports On Licit and Illicit Drugs." I loved her dearly for it. Every Friday night, I would reach for that book and disappear for the evening into topless bars and sometimes after-hours joints. I simply wanted to remain in that state of blissful intoxication forever. Only at best, I crashed straight through that state an into some place of emotional disability, of something that felt like living rigamortis, with a scathingly painful self consciousness: expose me to the light of day and I felt as if I would simply burst into flames and die.

Going to work was a chore. I hated the degree to which I felt self-conscious: everyone was paying attention to me. That was the cocaine. It escalated the pre-existing condition of narcissistic delusion and self-absorption -- the addiction to "self" to identifying with one's own thinking, to the point that I sometimes felt unable to leave the house, as if I would break under scrutiny of my fellow human beings. If I could have simply disappeared into a bottle, I would have.

My school held onto me. Why? I couldn't tell you. I had potential, my heart was in the right place, and I worked twice as hard as anyone had a right to in order make up for my deficits and transgressions. It was exhausting. I would overwork myself for days, sometimes weeks at a time, until I could no longer stand it, and then I would binge to forget the horror and pain of what I was and to relieve the stress of that kind of existence. What I never quite got as an alcoholic is that I was driven by self-loathing; almost every action I took depleted my emotional reservoir, which lead me right back to a drink: "I am a failure, a shameful and pitiful excuse for a human being. If I achieve enough, I can distance myself from this reality -- if only temporarily." It's like being in orbit, only not knowing it. I'd keep circling around and around, doing the same things again and again.

My behavior would run through the gamut of seasons: I'd drink until my body and psyche couldn't stand it any more; I'd spend longer and longer amounts of time recovering from the physical and psychological damage I'd done; I'd begin to feel better and work at life reasonably well, with the thought of perhaps having a drink as a sweet reward; I'd work extra hard to distance myself from my irresponsibility, putting in longer hours, more effort to make up for my transgressions; I'd begin to obsess over drinking and getting high again, driving myself even harder until I couldn't stand it. Then I'd drink. I was driven by an inside imbalance, but I kept searching for an outside solution.

I met people while on week long binges who had crossed over into lives of desperation that I simply drifted in and out of. These individuals could not hold a job, complete an education, manage to pay rent: they were either on the street or close to it. I kept joining them every time I drank. And then I would crawl back to the classroom. Sometimes it required three or four days of not drinking before I could bring myself back.

One day, I simply couldn't return. I turned on the gas in my apartment, cracked open a Corona and turned on the television. I had been drinking and snorting coke for nearly a week straight. I felt consumed by shame. Early in the week when I could still speak, I had called the job to let them know I wasn't coming to work, but eventually I stopped bothering with that. The early mornings from an evening with too much cocaine had left me unable to form words and sentences.

At one point, the walls of the room began to disappear. I saw shadowy figures lined up in growing multitudes, deepening in numbers where walls once stood. They were stolid creatures, standing still and emotionless, simply watching. I felt a peace coming over me. The phone rang. It was a topless dancer whom I had met earlier that week. She asked what I was doing. I told "nothing". Little else was said. I guess I was supposed to invite her over. I had gotten a divorce two years prior and now lived alone in an apartment for several months as my girlfriend had left. When I got off the phone, I shut off the gas. I no longer felt like dying immediately. I even opened a window. I still didn't feel much like living, but I wasn't going out that way.

The next day I rented a car and while it was a brutal struggle to get out of the apartment and go through any formal procedure that involved talking to other human beings, I managed it. I then drove as far as the first rest stop north of NYC. As badly as I wanted to drink, I knew I couldn't. If I did, then I'd never get where I was going. Where I was going was a whole 'nother story. I had some crazy idea of renting a room someplace in the mountains and drinking myself to death.

By late afternoon, I had arrived in the Catskills, at a beautifully situated motel at the bottom of a valley not far from the Ashokan Reservoir. The woman behind the counter looked suspiciously at me.

She asked me, "Do you smoke? I don't allow smoking in the rooms."

I told her, "No." And then I took a chance. "But I do drink. I'm quiet about it though."

Her face grew dark and she looked at me for a long time. Then she said, "Okay."

I paid her for two months in advance. My father had died and left me some money. The rest I got from credit card advances. There was a liquor store, a supermarket and a pizzeria all within a short walk of my room. And there was a pub across the street. While I still had my rented car, I drove into town and purchased a word processor on a credit card that I opened up at Sears. I also brought all the ink the store had and reams of paper. I decided that I would at least pursue one of my dreams, which was to write. Of course I stopped by the liquor store and purchased a case of vodka and many bottles of wine.

I drank whenever I wanted. I would wake up at 4:00 am, turn on the television, and when I realized that there was simply no reason for not drinking, I would pour myself a large glass of vodka, add a significant amount of crystal light to it and then drink with impunity. It was a wonderfully sickening life.

At one point, the family that ran the motel, which included an art gallery featuring their son's work, left for a week. It was the dead of winter and only I, their sole occupant, and the girl who cleaned the rooms, remained. I drank freely and liberally, tossing my empty wine and vodka bottles into a 100 gallon recycle bucket 50 yards from the room. Near the end of that week, I looked into the bucket once and noticed that it had grown quite full. Then I surveyed its contents: only my empty double sized wine bottles and liters of vodka were in that garbage pail. It dawned on me: there wasn't anyone else staying here, and in simply one week, I had consumed dozens of bottles of alcohol. It seemed inconceivable. My only thought was the hope that the recycle collection occurred before the owners returned.

I had heard the stories of my grandfather, who supposedly drank a full gallon of homemade wine for lunch every day. As with a lot of things I had heard in my house growing up, it remained in my memory, but it existed as a family fiction.

One day I had questioned my father about the legendary drinking of my grandfather.

"Oh yeah, Grandpa drank a full gallon of wine every single day for lunch."

"The homemade stuff?"

"Oh yeah."

"The entire gallon?"

"Yeah."

"Are you sure he drank the entire gallon? That homemade wine is pretty strong, next to poison."

At this, my father chuckled. And then he told me a story about himself – something he rarely ever did. "I was a kid back then, and we lived in Little Italy on Broome street. In the basement, Grandpa kept the barrels of wine he made. I had to go downstairs and tap the barrel, filling up an entire gallon. And then I had to carry it up all seven flights of stairs. And if I didn't fill the gallon to the top, he got angry with me and would send me back down."

"How long was lunch?"

"Oh, well, he'd sit for about two hours."

"He had a two hour lunch."

"Yeah. I would be playing in the street and the men would come and ask me, 'Where is your father.' In Italian. And I would tell them, 'Upstairs finishing his lunch.'"

"And what happened?"

"They'd wait around for a little while, and eventually they'd always go upstairs and get him."

"Get him to do what?"

"To go back to work."

"In that condition?"

"Two of them would help him down the stairs. Then they'd slip him up behind the wheel of the truck."

"They let him drive?"

My father laughed out loud, his stingy, controlled, drum roll of a snicker. "It was his truck. Those men worked for him."

"And he drove like that?"

"Yeah."

So when I began to easily consume two double bottles of wine a day, with glasses of vodka in the morning and evenings, I realized that while I hadn't yet reached my grandfather's prodigious drinking levels, I had certainly moved into his neighborhood.

One day I had had enough. Six weeks of heavy drinking had left me pretty insane. I remember preparing a Thanksgiving dinner for myself on a Wednesday night, when the girl who cleaned up came in and asked me what I was doing for Thanksgiving, if I had a place to go. She was extending an invitation to me to eat with her and her family. I calmly explained to her that I had it under control, and while I deeply appreciated her kindness, that I, as she could see, had already begun my cooking for the holiday. She nervously pointed out that Thanksgiving wasn't for another week. I was horrified. I had completely lost track of time. The landlady later put it this way: you really have stepped out of the world and forgotten about it. And I had.

It took a full two weeks into my stay up there before I first laughed again. I looked back on the life I had run away from and I felt such relief not to be living it anymore. There was the teaching responsibilities, which had grown so large that they encroached upon my sanity. I felt eaten up emotionally, never finding enough time to choose the right words to tell my students exactly what would help them. There was the divorce and the move and the separation from my son, only six at the time, and the love of a younger woman – none of which I could fully process. These things, too, ate away at me. I could not find myself in all of this, so I had run to silence the painful and haunting voices that spoke shamefully of my decisions, mounting them as failures. My inability to meet life head on, to fulfill responsibilities that I had chosen, told the story of the failure of the man, whom I had always been.

I turned to the drink, which really is a flight from reality. Under the influence of alcohol, I could tell myself a different story. Those people who ate at me through their incessant expectations –

expectations I could never fully meet – were better off without me, and I certainly was better off without them. My own failed expectations – expectations that spoke to me in the voices of all the people I knew people -- haunted me. The voices of my in laws, and my colleagues, my administrators and my landlord, my ex girlfriend and my ex wife -- the list went on. From time to time, they became the voices of my mother and my sister and my father, of the neighbors back when I was growing up and from the family of the first girl whom I had ever loved. They were always accusatory voices.

With the drink inside of me, life grew simple: I needed to eat and drink. Television did the rest. If nothing worthwhile was on, I could write. Any time I woke up, it was okay to drink, to write, to watch tv, and anytime I felt like it, it was okay to sleep and eat and do absolutely nothing. And in this way I remained for six full weeks.

The money began to run short, and while I could secure more, I could see that alcohol would not get the job done. I thought perhaps I would go into the woods and simply stay there. I had camping equipment.

The late autumn days had become bursts of color in a valley that stood between two places: to my right lay the place from whence I had come, and to my left loomed the uncertain future. I hired a cab to drop me on the roadside with my camping equipment and my luggage. People know when you're crazy. They just don't actually know what to do about it. They might ask you a few questions, but really most prefer to leave you alone as some part of them reasonably fears that your "crazy" will end up directed toward them.

I hiked up into the mountains with backpack on and hauling a huge suitcase. I made it more than a full mile up the mountain before I moved as far off the trail as I reasonably could. Over the past five years, I had become 40 pounds overweight from the drinking, overeating and inactivity, so the hike up the mountain was no easy feat. It was cold and it had begun snowing. My camping equipment, tent, and sleeping bag were designed for the late Spring and Summer.

I began to feel unusually warm. Setting up the tent was easy, and I put all my belongings inside of it. Outside, I removed my shirt and stood shivering and sweating, opening my mouth at the sky to take in the snowflakes. They fell out of the growing darkness, which then disappeared as a giant moon rose over the side of the mountain, lighting up the night. Light snow continued to fall, and the moon took up the southern sky like another planet coming into being.

I felt pain I had never known fully, with no alcohol along to numb me. I couldn't understand why my body seemed so warm although I wore no shirt. For sure, I should be freezing to death, but I wasn't.

I began speaking to God. It started quietly at first, bits of sentences.

"I'm here, now God. So this is it. I'm done."

I continued for a while looking up at that vast expanse where flakes fell like infinity, and I and the sky moved as one. Before I knew it, I was yelling up at the sky, at God. "Take me. I know you're out there. I know you've watched the whole thing. I've failed. You hear me, I failed? Okay. I admit it. I'm giving up. I'm tossing in my cards. You take me now."

Nothing answered. I felt enraged with terror and shame, so I began to scream up at the sky, at God. "YOU TAKE ME NOW GOD! I'M FINISHED! I'M DONE! DO YOU UNDERSTAND ME!! I KNOW YOU'RE OUT THERE LISTENING SO YOU TAKE ME BECAUSE I CAN'T DO THIS ANYMORE."

And then it happened. I heard them. Footsteps. Large crunching footsteps. At first, I felt embarrassed and ashamed. Someone had actually heard me in my desperate and humiliating craziness.

The footsteps grew larger and louder. I could tell that whatever it was, was definitely on two feet and it was coming toward me now. I stood still without my shirt, the snowflakes still coming.

I wondered whether it was the owner of the land adjacent to the state property that I was on. Who else would be wandering around at night in the dark? I struggled to look around, but I saw nothing: no light, no movement of any kind.

The footsteps continued, this time somehow larger, moving directly, I was sure, toward me. Whatever it was, it was huge. The crushing down of branches and the crackling of dried leaves told me that. Louder and louder the footsteps grew. I was shivering in the cold, paralyzed by a fear I had never known. This thing that came towards me in the dark had a presence that I could sense: not only was it huge and powerful, but it was coming for me. All those years of martial arts went right out the window. What now lumbered toward me, deliberate and methodical in its approach, terrified me. The steps grew increasingly loud as this thing, which I still could not see, grew closer and closer. I could practically hear it breathing; I could sense its immensity.

And then it stopped just outside of my vision, standing there in the dark, waiting. For the longest time, I could not move for fear it would rush out of the darkness the moment I revealed my position and pounce upon me. Finally, stiff from the cold, I got myself back into the tent. I lay nearly frozen, listening.

All night long I lay awake listening, freezing slowly. In the morning, I could hear voices along the stream. Perhaps it was the stream. I could almost make out what was being said, and I knew had I stayed any longer that I would begin to understand the voices of the stream. And I would follow those voices to their source. And I would be lost forever.

I stood up outside the tent, unusually stiff. My limbs gave way and I fell over in the snow. I stood up again and almost fell a second time. It was time to go. I packed the one large suitcase, leaving the camping equipment. And I made my way down the trail, falling frequently in places I shouldn't have fallen. The voices of the stream called me back, speaking to me. I paused once or twice to listen, but I knew if I stayed too long, I would turn and follow them back up the mountain, never to return.

I had prayed before I headed down – although I'm not a religious man. I prayed because things had happened on this trip to teach me that there are forces beyond my understanding, which were at work in my life. So I prayed, "God, help me get down from this mountain." In the night, while I had lain awake, some part of me had hoped someone I knew would come to rescue me, but no one came. I was alone. So I prayed. And I prayed because of the one thing that had happened while I was at the motel, which I couldn't shake from my mind.

I had been drinking excessively again, and in order to continue to get drunk, I would have to vomit. I frequently had to vomit, both in the morning and at different points in the day and evening in order to keep drinking. I feared the owner, a religious woman, would have me thrown from the place if she heard me vomiting violently, so I tried to manage it quietly, but this evening they were in the office so I decided to walk back into the woods and throw up as far away from the room as I could possibly get.

I started off by walking through the thick underbrush. Branches and bushes cut across my face and arms as I moved. I felt it coming, so I began to hurry because I hadn't gotten far enough from the office where the owners now sat. As I picked up my pace, I felt the mounting shame of all my failures driving me: my failed marriage, my failed teaching career, my failed bid to live independently, my failed attempt at being a single father, my failed "other woman" relationship that was supposed to redeem me. I began to run blindly through the woods, driven by these demons, branches lashing my face, arms, and legs wildly like whips. And then I was stopped dead on a dime by a set of glowing eyes looking back at me through the darkness. I froze for a moment until my vision cleared up. In front of me just a dozen yards or so stood a beautiful deer poised directly in the middle of a large clearing, the light from a bright and nearly full moon shining down like a beacon from God. The deer's eyes were afire with this light. A moment or so passed, and my vision cleared up just a bit more: Less than four inches from my neck strung tautly between two trees hung a thin strand of barbed wire. Had I taken one full step more, I would have slit my own throat.

So I prayed as I made my way down the mountain, nearly unconscious from hyperthermia but fully unaware of that fact. I just kept comically falling down – until I made it to the side of the road. Almost immediately, a car pulled over. I must have looked like a sight.

"So what are you doing here?" a woman asked, her passenger window partially rolled down.

"Camping."

She looked at me doubtfully as I sat on my suitcase. "With luggage?"

"I had to leave the camping gear back in the woods."

"No one comes by this road at this time." She said to me.

"I didn't know that."

"I never pick up hitchhikers."

"I understand."

"But get in."

"Thank you."

And I got in. She took me as far as the crossroads off the major highway where I got another ride easily.

Back at the motel, I realized that I would live. And part of me had begun to want to live again – not the way that I had lived, but some simpler way where I wouldn't drive myself crazy. For seven full days, I couldn't shut my eyes without seeing some other insane world that pulled at me. I didn't drink, and I couldn't sleep, not even for a minute. At the end of a full week, I closed my eyes and slept again. And then I started drinking once more.

I called the VA hospital and the counselor told me I was in bad company. I thought he must have misunderstood that I was alone. "Yes," he explained. "You're alone with an alcoholic." I told him I would be down by the end of the month. A severe rainstorm held me for an additional four days, but I eventually made it back to Brooklyn and to the VA hospital where I slowly got better.

From there, I checked into a therapeutic community called "Samaritan Village." It was a program for dually addicted homeless veterans. As I was an alcoholic and a cocaine addict who was now homeless (My VA patient ID actually said, "Homeless" on it.), this program accommodated me. Nine months later, I found myself back in the classroom teaching – even though I was still living in this locked facility and on public assistance. I have to be the only teacher in NYC ever to be on welfare while teaching – and locked up. They'd release me in the morning to go to work, and I'd get locked up again in the evening every night, lying in a room with seven other guys. It was a humbling experience. And I was still homeless.

It took until the second month of teaching for me to actually get a place in Brooklyn, and I had to use my ex-wife as a reference. She was good about the whole thing, and another guy I had been in rehab with who owned a home in Sheepshead Bay acted as a second reference. He claimed a fire in his home had burned up all my belongings, which explained why I came there with absolutely nothing.

Now, during my eighth year away from that entire experience, I wanted to run, to escape again. One day, after an AA meeting where everyone told me how good I sounded despite my pleading in desperation during my share about how I simply couldn't go on, I began drinking again. I lasted less than a month into the teaching year before I ended up at a motel in upstate NY for more than six weeks, followed by a trip to the VA hospital in Albany – only this time I ended up in the psych ward with a blood alcohol count of .35, which wasn't even close to the hospital record.

I couldn't sleep the first night, and my psychotic roommate spent the entire night packing and unpacking his bags while wildly talking to himself. When he finally put his suitcase down on my bed, I asked him, "What the hell are you doing?" He apologized and continued more quietly until morning.

I had been unraveling at the job -- as well as at home -- and I knew it. As the dean, I had harshly scolded one girl for violating a young man by throwing his jacket into the garbage after I had specifically warned both of them to stay away from each other.

"It doesn't matter what you say." I remember telling her. "I saw you throw his jacket into the dumpster. You were told to stay away from him." I could see that my colleagues thought that I was being harsh.

"Oh my god!" I remember her exclaiming and then running around the classroom until she vomited into a trash can. "I can't believe you're doing this to me." And she vomited again. I felt horrible but I didn't budge.

At night, my wife and I were taking turns staying up with our newborn. Neither of us slept at all. Each morning, I had to drop my four year old off at daycare 30 minutes away on the other side of the Bronx, then drive south for another 30 minutes and drop off my newborn at my mother-in-law's, only she almost never answered the door because of some mixture of medications she was taking. I could bang for 15 minutes straight with no answer. I worried that her neighbors would shoot me for making that kind of noise each morning.

Once, I actually gave up, parked the car -- no easy feat in itself as that could take another 30 minutes just to find a spot -- and then came back to bang on the door for another 15 minutes. After dropping off the little guy, I took the train yet another 30 minutes into the city to get to work, and then repeated the entire thing in reverse. Every morning. Every evening. How other people do these things is beyond me. I simply couldn't. I felt as if my responsibilities had swallowed me, and I could no longer breathe.

I fed my children dinner and then marked papers and passed out or not, depending whether or not I had baby duty that night. When I had baby duty, I lay on the couch, rocking the little guy in his car-like seat while I closed my eyes and listened to him cry then not cry. Sometimes I held him and just cried with him.

Just outside of the city on a Sunday, I confessed this to my wife in the parking lot of a supermarket as afternoon darkened into evening.

"I can't do this anymore."

"You'll get through this."

"You don't understand. I feel like taking you and the kids out of the car right now and then driving and never coming back. Both boys were sleeping in the back. I can't do this anymore."

"You can."

I couldn't.

That week, I began drinking on my way home from work. A week later, I left NYC and drank for nearly seven weeks straight. Then I entered the rehab, driven up to Albany by the same cab driver who took me on coke runs back to the Bronx every week. When I cleared up enough to speak with a psychiatrist, I tearfully told him everything. "No one would listen. I just couldn't do it any more. I had begged my wife, 'Hold off on buying the house. You're pregnant and I'm starting a new job in July. Let's wait another year. Please. It's too much change.'"

The psychiatrist told me I wasn't crazy. I was astounded.

"You look disappointed."

"Did you hear what I told you?"

"Yes. You had a breakdown. That's it. But you're not crazy."

"Not crazy."

"Look around you." I was in the psych ward detoxing. "There's plenty of crazy here. You are definitely not crazy."

Before I left the psych ward, one of the patients told me, "Listen, Joe. You were able to get along in here with all of us and you're not like us. Look around you. People are really fucked up in here, but we all can recognize that you're different. The fact that you could get along with us without any problems, that's gotta count for something." He shook my hand. "Good luck." And after that complete clarity, he wandered off in his usual psychotic schtick.

Ten days later, I was in rehab. Three months later, I was teaching again. And I managed to stay sober this time until the month before I retired, which was more than nine years later.

This time I didn't go back to AA. There had been five two or three day binges over a five month period of time, with a full month of "controlled" drinking where I consumed a bottle of wine five days a week for an entire month -- all ending in a 13 day binge. And then I went for a different kind of help. I went holistic.

Three months of immersive treatment followed where I attended psychotherapeutic groups, reiki, yoga, meditation, acupuncture, art therapy, sand therapy, music therapy, equine therapy, individual and group counseling and the magical EMDR. I dropped AA and decided not to divorce my wife and leave my family, which was probably the unfortunate mistake. But I couldn't leave my family.

I discovered that I had suffered from severe and sustained childhood trauma, and until I treated those wounds and began the healing process, I had no shot of ever living a happy, balanced life. What I didn't know was I couldn't continue to heal in an unsafe environment, which is what I had cocreated in my home over the past decade and a half. And that the marriage couldn't be salvaged.

I also discovered that when I continued to treat the underlying condition through yoga and mindful meditation, journaling the entire experience, my alcoholism left me alone. And those nasty rages I often flew into when I was sober, which I couldn't explain or control and felt deep shame over, they went away too. It hadn't been my "alcoholic thinking" that was troubling me; it had been trauma and ungrieved wounds that drove my behavior. I'd used alcohol and drugs to alleviate the shame and self-loathing that lay at the core of my wounded self. Once I exposed the wounds and the thinking that lay hidden behind the events which had caused the trauma, replacing it with more reasonable understandings, I found that I could cope with life and other people without any kind of medication at all. I was amazed. It was far from perfect, but it remained light years away from what I had been.

AA, while it had helped keep the drink out of my hands, had somehow communicated to me through its participants that if I failed to get better, the failure was on me. I had repeatedly tried therapy and medication while in AA. Everything worked for a while, and then didn't work: Years and years of struggling, only to fall back on myself. I learned in AA that one definition of insanity was doing the same thing again and again but expecting different results. Going back to AA again and again and expecting different results had been insanity for me. My therapists confirmed that I had needed a different and deeper kind of treatment and that all the AA in the world wouldn't have kept me from flying into rages, fleeing from my home and family and job even while sober -- something I had frequently done over the last nine years of my sobriety -- and eventually, no matter what I had done, I would have drunk again. Or worse. Who knew?

It wasn't as if I had suddenly been cured. Inside, it was as if the broken pieces of who I had been were suddenly put back on the playing field. Instead of this emotional fist exploding into my consciousness every time the trauma got triggered, driving me into fight or flight mode, I now had a chance. I saw the fingers of this fist of feelings that had wrapped themselves around each other: shame, rage, anger, guilt, fear, self loathing, once coiled together as one, now uncurling, just enough to allow in the light of compassion, of forgiveness. From then on, I rarely felt blindsided by explosions of unfathomable emotion. I have felt overwhelmed by my own pain or sense of inadequacy; over time, I've learned to work with the person that I am. While I still sometimes feel some of the pain, of the inadequacy, even the shame that once ruled me, it no longer overwhelms me to the point that I run from my life for any length of time or do things that ruin my life or deeply harm others.

It's difficult to sit with my feelings and watch as I begin to tell myself stories about the pain. It's even harder to listen to the stories I do tell -- have told myself for as long as I can remember. In the middle of meditation, I find myself weeping; sometimes, alone on the mat in yoga, I am crying to the point that I can't breathe. Afterwards, I always feel cleansed. I watch the part of me that wants it all to be over, to finish. And I've come to know how harsh and unforgiving I am of myself. Healing has become a journey into self compassion and forgiveness.

Chapter Fifteen

Endings

"Bad news. Yonny got shot. Doesn't look good. Thought you'd want to know."

Yonny had been my student for the better part of four years. I got the news of the shooting from a colleague who was about to retire. I myself had retired nearly a year and a half earlier.

I visited him in the hospital where I needed to get permission to enter his room from his mother who immediately recognized me. We'd met at a hospital once before when Yonny had had his finger run over while ice skating -- a nasty cut resulting in several stitches but no real damage.

While I had been told no one would be allowed in the room, his mom, Sylvia, went in alone and asked Yonny if he wanted to see me. Then she waved me in. He recognized me and responded to everything I said although he couldn't speak because of tube down his throat. He still had two of the bullets in him: one in the back of the neck, which would probably leave him paralyzed for the rest of his life and one in his abdomen. Doctors were waiting for him to get stronger and for the bullet in his neck to possibly shift.

I felt surprised by how strong he looked. It gave me hope. At the time, I was doing volunteer work for the veteran's hospital, and

I'd just seen a man who had been paralyzed from the waist down walk past me in the hallway through the use of some advanced technologies. I figured that 10 years down the road, even if Yonny ended up paralyzed, new technologies would present themselves and he might one day walk again. Except for his swollen legs, he seemed present, responsive but perhaps a little tired. While I wanted to, I couldn't bring myself to place my hands on him.

He died the next day.

I went to his wake and was asked to give a four minute speech at that June's graduation about Yonny. He had been an advisee of mine, and we had been close. He could be a bit brutal at times, especially with the girls, and some of his sexual exploits spoke to that -- stories I'd been reluctant ever to repeat aloud if they'd happened to me -- but mostly he was warm and supportive and caring.

At the graduation ceremony, the principal introduced me and explained how I'd been Yonny's advisor. This is what I said:

"Having to endure the loss of your own child is a most unnatural act, and it is the single greatest fear I have as a parent. Sylvia, I'm sorry for your unimaginable loss.

My colleagues have reminded me that I nicknamed Yonny the Mayor of REACH because even after he graduated he was here so often and he always knew more about what was going on around the school than I did. I used to say, "Where you'd find that out." He'd say, "Oh, yeah. Trust me." And he'd nod his head. I had to call down to the office one time and check on something he was telling me. And then I said to him, "How are you finding out all this stuff?" He just smiled that big smile he used to have.

"Yonny could be warm and he treated us like family and he always liked us to do things together. It was important to him. He supported this sense of community we have here. One time we went bowling and he threw a 16 pound bowling ball ⅔ of the way down the alley in the air before it before hit the ground and knocked all the pins down. I thought, "Damn, this guy is strong."

"To have someone taken from us, it leaves such a hole in our lives. We don't know what another person will do throughout his life, we don't know what course he will take, how many other lives he'll touch, and we don't know what kind of hole he'll leave in the

community, in the family, in the individuals who loved him until he is gone.

"Something I don't talk about: My first 15 years of teaching I lost a student every single year to violence on the streets. One guy, about two weeks before he died, I was talking with him about some things in his journal where he had written about how dangerous it was out on the streets. This kid was brilliant. At his funeral, one of my colleagues said that he could have been the next Malcolm X.

"We don't know who a person could have become when they are taken away from the rest of us; we don't know whose lives they could have touched and what differences they would have made. We don't know who may have needed Yonny's warmth and support in this uncertain world, what his kindness and love may have done for someone he never had the chance to meet.

"I had another kid, maybe my 18th year of teaching, he was in a short story class, and when he was killed for his coat, we agonized over whether or not we should finish his story for him. In the end, we dedicated the collection of stories to him, and what we said was, "We left this story unfinished, like his life."

Yonny's life was unfinished.

"Will Connell, whom I shared an office with for many years, said that an old cat once told him the difference between his generation and this generation: "My generation wasn't afraid to die; this generation isn't afraid to kill."

"Life is hard enough. No one has the right to take away the people we love, our brothers and sisters, our husbands and wives, our children. I've looked into the eyes of parents who have lost a child. It is a wound you never recover from.

"You want to remember Yonny. The next time you feel like hurting someone, the next time you feel like placing yourself or someone else in danger, stop yourself.

"We are are like drops of water in this sea of humanity, touching each other's lives in ways none of us can fully understand. When any of us commits an act of violence, we poison that pool.

"Look at the number of people in this room. The average person interacts with 100,000 different people over the course of a lifetime. Think about how many lives we'll touch But not Yonny. His life was cut short. There are 70,000 people who will never get to know him, even if only for a brief instance of kindness or a look of warmth.

His family had him stolen from them. We have lost this man forever because someone didn't understand that he was a son, a brother and a friend.

"I miss you, Yonny, and it hurts that you're gone."

At the graduation, I saw students who'd taken classes with me about to graduate, one who had already landed a job with the school, former colleagues who struggled with the work I could no longer do, and my former bosses who had me sit with them. I knew I would never teach again, never do this kind of work. I had given, though most imperfectly, all that I had to give along these lines, and now it was time to rest.

What can you say about teaching? It's one of the toughest things you'll ever do well. It requires at times that you give all of yourself, muster up infinite patience, forgive and understand when all that you've given seems to have amounted to nothing, move on again and again, constantly reinventing yourself; motivate others when you can hardly motivate yourself out of the bed, let go of the results, irrespective of how powerful they may seem at the time to make room to do it all again until the next bell signals your time has ended. I am grateful that my life has been given the meaning derived from having taught and been taught by what might be considered those who have lost their way as I, too, have lost mine too many times.

In the end, I had found my way back home, but only for a little while. I relapsed two more times, went for holistic treatment for the underlying issues, dropped AA, therapy, medication, and found myself meditating, practicing t'ai chi and yoga. My wife commented that had she not seen the changes in me, she would have never believed that they were possible. My counselor from after care in Florida wrote to me in an email that I had transcended AA. And then I relapsed again. And again.

Finally, I found a compassionate path to healing and change through a Buddhist approach to recovery from addiction, compulsivity, codependency, and trauma. After nearly three decades of trying to care for and help others, I found the ways to care for and help myself -- something I had always told my students: what you're doing with your life has to work for you. Though there have been bumps in the road, I'm still on this path today. May each of you find and honor your own paths. Namaste.

About the Author

The author was raised in Brooklyn, NY during the 1960's and 70's. From the early 60's to the mid 70's, his neighborhood went from a safe place where children played openly in the streets to a violent, drug and crime infested war zone. During his first semester of college, in an effort to avoid being drawn further in to that street life, he joined the military where he became a police officer. After he was honorably discharged, he finished his education, completing a Masters Degree in English/Secondary Education from City College. He tried his hand at 26 different jobs before he ended up teaching high school to inner city youth for more than a quarter of a century. He now lives upstate New York where he regularly hikes the Catskill mountains.

Publisher's Note

The contents of this book are Patrick Nichols' personal memoirs of how he experienced and interpreted the events detailed. They are in no way meant to be a historical accounting. Names and other identifiers have been changed. The thoughts, opinions and recollections in no way represent those of the publisher or the forementioned institutions. That said, we at Volossal encourage the reader to research any and all claims made in this book as well as any other claims and accusations regarding the educational system in the United States. We felt it was extremely important that Patrick Nichols' story be told in the hopes of shining a light on a very flawed system. It is our hope that this books is a step toward reform and improvement.

www.ingramcontent.com/pod-product-compliance
Lightning Source LLC
Chambersburg PA
CBHW032043150426
43194CB00006B/397